When RUGBY *Was* RUGBY

First published in 2013

A catalogue record for this book is available from the British Library

ISBN: 978-0-85733-187-8

Published by Haynes Publishing, Sparkford, Yeovil,
Somerset BA22 7JJ, UK
Tel: 01963 442030 Fax: 01963 440001
Int. tel: +44 1963 442030 Int. fax: +44 1963 440001
E-mail: sales@haynes.co.uk
Website: www.haynes.co.uk

Haynes North America Inc., 861 Lawrence Drive,
Newbury Park, California 91320, USA

Images © Mirrorpix

Creative Director: Kevin Gardner
Designed for Haynes by BrainWave

Printed and bound in the US

When RUGBY *Was* RUGBY

The Story of Home Nations Rugby Union

Neil Palmer

Contents

4   Foreword

6   Birth of a Sport   1823-1910

14   The Five Nation Rivals   1910-1999

82   The Lions

116   Rivals Across the Sea: "The Tourists"

140   The Baa Baas

150   Fields of Dreams

164   Blood, Sweat, Tears, Laughter and Royals

184   The Modern Game   1987-2013

Foreword

I would like to thank Haynes Publishing, the *Daily Mirror* and Neil Palmer for inviting me to contribute to this wonderful book, which brings back so many memories through the *Daily Mirror*'s extraordinary photo archive.

When I look back on my life in rugby there is nothing I would rather have done than play this great game. From the moment I pulled on the not-so-famous jersey of Longlevens Secondary Modern School in Gloucester I was hooked. The master in charge was Dennis Williams, and he wasted no time in telling me that I was a prop. Years later, and now a regular in Gloucester's first team, I asked Dennis what made him place me as prop. "Burton," he replied, "Rugby Union caters for all shapes and sizes. It's an inclusive game which provides opportunities for a wide range of abilities." He went on, "Remember inside every prop is an outside half trying to get out. But please don't get carried away because you were a prop when you started and you will be a prop when you finish." With those words he reflected the culture of rugby, a game that keeps you grounded and never too far above your station.

As a young boy I watched Gloucester from the famous shed, and I can remember the basic courtesy amongst opposing players, who never failed to shake hands at the end of the game and applaud each other as they left the field. The fabric of the game has not changed and its "spirit" has been captured in this book. Rugby has done so much for me, from the moment I made my Gloucester debut at the tender age of 18, to my adventures with England, the Barbarians and the very pinnacle of the game – the British and Irish Lions.

The pictures in this book demonstrate clearly how rugby has changed. English and Welsh clubs now play in different leagues and only meet in European competitions. I much regret the passing of the midweek cross-border games that

Gloucester used to play against the Welsh clubs such as Cardiff, Pontypool and Llanelli. They were tough battles and the fans loved them. On a worldwide scale the game has never been more popular. There is no more mystique about the huge forwards and speed merchants who arrive here from the southern hemisphere because now we see them every weekend on Sky TV, which has opened a global window on the game. We are seeing the likes of Canada, the USA and Russia continuing to make progress, along with Japan, who are staging the Rugby World Cup in 2019.

When Rugby Was Rugby has enabled me to read about some of the legends I faced in opposition, as well as those who stood shoulder to shoulder alongside me in the heat of battle. May I offer my congratulations to everyone involved in the creation of this unique pictorial record of the game I love.

MIKE BURTON
Gloucester, England, Barbarians, British And Irish Lions

Birth of a Sport
1823-1910

> *In 1823 William Webb Ellis first picked up the ball and ran with it. And for the next 156 years forwards have been trying to work out why.*
>
> Sir Tasker Watkins (1979) President of the WRU

When
RUGBY was
RUGBY

There have been many different versions of how this great game of rugby came to be born. We know that it has its roots in Association Football, and, if we go back in time, every nation had a very similar version of the sport.

The Romans played a game called "Harpastum" in which two teams competed to throw a large ball into an opposing goal. Medieval Irishmen played "Cad", which involved carrying an inflated bladder into goals that were created by bending trees into an arch. The Welsh had a game called "Cnapan", in which teams would fight for a wooden ball and attempt to carry it away from the opposition.

It's clear that rugby originated from a mixture of all these pursuits – as with most games, it evolved through time. But whether it's true or not, the tale that appears throughout the history books is that, in 1823 at Rugby School in England, a pupil called William Webb Ellis picked the ball up during a game of football and ran with it, and from this the wonderful game of rugby was born. From that one moment public schools throughout England developed their own version of the game. As it grew in popularity the sport was standardized, along with rules – and the rest, as they say, is history.

Rugby Union on the playing fields of Rugby School – where it all began.

1823 Tale of William Webb Ellis picking up the ball in a game at Rugby School, England. 1845 First rules introduced. 1850 Rubber is used instead of a pig's bladder to standardize the ball. 1863 Parting of the ways between rugby and Association Football. 1871 The Rugby Union formed at Pall Mall in London. The first ever rugby international held between England and Scotland. 1874 The Irish Rugby Union formed. 1875 Ireland's first ever international, as Ireland take on England at the Oval in London. 1878 The Calcutta Cup is presented to the victors of the game between England and Scotland for the first time. 1881 Welsh Rugby Union formed. Wales play England in their first international. 1883 The Home International tournament – between the four home countries – is devised. 1885 Referees are allowed whistles in games. 1886 The Scottish Rugby Union formed. 1890 Points scoring system is changed to allow two points for a penalty and three points for a "try". Scotland and England share the Home International title. 1895 Due to the demand for northern teams to pay players, they break away and form the Northern Union, which will become the Rugby League. 1897 Numbers are placed on jerseys. 1900 Wales dominate the Home Internationals, winning six titles in the next 10 years.

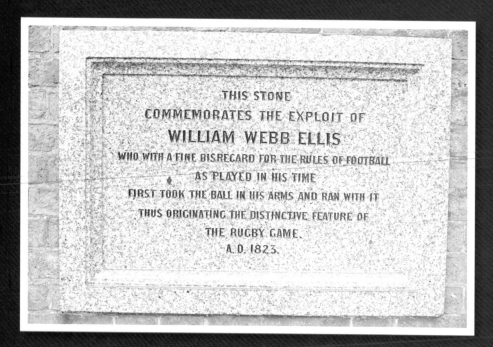

THIS STONE
COMMEMORATES THE EXPLOIT OF
WILLIAM WEBB ELLIS
WHO WITH A FINE DISREGARD FOR THE RULES OF FOOTBALL
AS PLAYED IN HIS TIME
FIRST TOOK THE BALL IN HIS ARMS AND RAN WITH IT
THUS ORIGINATING THE DISTINCTIVE FEATURE OF
THE RUGBY GAME.
A.D. 1823.

LEFT: Plaque at Rugby School commemorating William Webb Ellis, who is alleged to have invented the sport of rugby. Born in Salford, Lancashire, Ellis attended Rugby School, Warwickshire, after moving to the area with his family. He attended the school from 1816 to 1825 and it is alleged that he caught the ball during a football match (which is allowed) but also ran with it – and so the legend was born. Ellis went on to be an Anglican clergyman. He never married and died in the south of France in 1872. Whether he did indeed start the game is up for debate, but he will be forever linked with the sport after the Rugby World Cup was named the "Webb Ellis Trophy" in 1987.

Coventry Rugby Club 1891. Coventry were one of the top English club teams in this new sport of rugby. In 1872 they were one of the first teams to follow the Scottish clubs and move from the 20-a-side game to the 15-a-side that we know today.

LEFT: Quality control at the Gilbert ball factory. In 1842 Richard Linden and William Gilbert started making rugby balls from pigs' bladders for Rugby School. This became a problem, as the size of the bladder was determined by the size of the pig. This meant the sizes of balls varied. The factory started to use rubber in 1862, which standardized the ball size. To this day, Gilbert's, as they are known, still make all the rugby balls for the International Rugby Board.

BELOW: Weighing the rugby balls by hand at the Gilbert ball factory. Today the balls are weighed by machine.

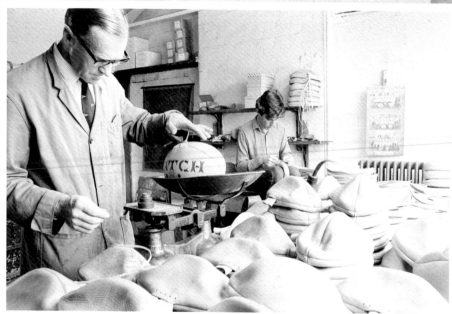

Manchester Rugby Union side, who were one of the biggest in England. They spearheaded the popularity of the game in the North of England. This photo dates from the 1877/78 season.

The Castle Hotel, Neath, Wales

The Castle Hotel was where the very first meeting of the Welsh Rugby Union was held – on 12th March 1881. The Union was devised so that the game could be regulated amongst the teams that were forming in Wales at the time. Unions in England, Ireland and Scotland were also forming at that time.

RESULTS OF THE 1905 MATCHES

WALES beat ENGLAND at Cardiff on Jan 14th by 2 Goals 5 Tries to nil. Try-getters: Morgan (2), Gabe (2), Llewellyn, Watkins and R Jones.
WALES beat SCOTLAND at Inverleith on Feb 4th by 2 Tries to 1 Try. Llewellyn scored the Welsh Tries, and Little scored for Scotland.
WALES beat IRELAND at Swansea on March 11th by 2 Goals to 1 Try. W Jones and E T Morgan scored the Welsh Tries, and George Davies kicked the Goals. Robinson made Ireland's Try.

3

> " Nowhere was the spirit of conquest and racial superiority so vigorously and selfishly kept alive as in the nations of the UK. "
>
> Historian R R Davies 1938–2005

The Five Nation Rivals
1910-1999

From 1871, when England first played Scotland in the very first international match, rivalry leapt off the battlefield of old and straight into the sporting arena. In 1910 France were invited to join the Home International tournament and the Five Nations was born.

Over the years, the competition has produced some of the greatest teams and players the game of rugby has ever seen. Throughout its magnificent history every nation has "had its day", a time when it dominated the other countries by producing a magnificent team, and, alternately, they have all shared lows when the wooden spoon was their only "prize" and thoughts immediately turned to next year's competition. The tournament has re-established countries' identities, which, in the modern world, can sometimes be forgotten, and lets fans revel in pride and passion for their nation – which is something that must never be lost.

1910 France invited to join the Five Nations. England dominates, winning five out of the next six tournaments. **1915** Competition stopped due to the First World War. **1920** The Five Nation teams lose 108 current internationals during the war. England continue to dominate, winning four titles in five years. **1925** Scotland wins the Grand Slam, and four titles in five years. **1930** France removed from tournament after paying players. **1931** Wales win the last Five Nations before France leave. **1932** Competition reverts back to Home Internationals. **1938** Scotland versus England becomes first game shown on TV. **1940** Competition stopped due to the Second World War. **1946** Four Nations lose 60 current internationals during the conflict. **1947** France invited back as Five Nations resumes. **1948** A great Ireland side dominate, winning three titles in four years. **1952** Wales win Grand Slam. **1955** Wales and France share title. **1959** France dominate, winning four titles back to back. **1964** Wales win three titles in a row. **1969** Wales dominate, with a legendary side, for the next 10 years. **1972** No tournament due to the Troubles in Northern Ireland. **1973** All five countries share title. **1980** England win the Grand Slam for the first time in 23 years. **1982** Ireland win Triple Crown for the first time in 33 years. **1986** France dominate, winning four titles back to back. **1990** Scotland win Grand Slam. **1991** Start of England dominance, as they win four titles in six years. **1997** France win back-to-back titles. **1999** Scotland win the last Five Nations title.

"The Early Years": Twenties, Thirties and Forties

The 1920s were a time when all the Home Nations shared success in the Championships, but England and Scotland were particularly strong, with England winning four Grand Slams during the decade and Scotland one. The Scots and English continued their success throughout the Thirties, but the end of the decade (after the Second World War) saw the emergence of Wales, and possibly one of the greatest teams of all time – the Irish team of 1948. Ireland would dominate the end of the Forties with a tremendous team led by the great Jack Kyle.

–LEGENDS–

Wavell Wakefield

Wavell Wakefield was more than just a rugby player. Apart from winning three Grand Slams with England in the 1920s he changed the face of rugby as we know it, by revolutionizing the pack and giving players, who had previously just played anywhere, individual roles. Born in Beckenham in Kent in 1898, he became an all-round sportsman, excelling in cricket and athletics. However, he loved the game of rugby, making his debut for his beloved Harlequins in 1919, then gaining his first England cap against Wales the following year. He was instrumental in England Grand Slam success during the following years, as they beat all before them. He captained England on 13 occasions, and stood down in 1926, after gaining 31 caps. On retirement he became a Conservative MP at the age of 37, and at the age of 46 received a knighthood. Wavell Wakefield was also president of the Rugby Football Union, and in 1963 became 1st Baron Wakefield. He died in Kendal in 1983 aged 85, but will always be remembered as the father of English rugby.

RUGBY –STATS–

Wavell Wakefield

Name: Wavell Wakefield

Born: Beckenham 1898

Country: England

Position: Flanker, Lock, Number 8

International Caps: 31

Clubs: Harlequins

Representative Honours: Barbarians

The Wales "Terrible Eight"

ABOVE: The Rev Alban Davies and his "Terrible Eight" of 1914 in Belfast. They fought their Irish adversaries in a private war that would be legendary within rugby.

Left to right, standing: Percy Jones, Edgar Morgan, Harry Uzzell, T C Lloyd, D Watts. Seated: Tom Williams, Rev Alban Davies, W E Rees (WRU secretary), Bedwellty Jones.

Apparently Irish players came to the Welsh team's hotel the night before the match. Ireland's pack leader, William Tyrrell, told Welsh forward Percy Jones in no uncertain terms what he was going to do to him in the match. Another Welsh forward responded by asking if "Anybody could join in?" Consequently, the scene was set for what has gone down as one of the roughest games ever played in the history of the Rugby Union. Players fought running battles with each other, whether they had the ball or not. Wales won the game 11-3 and in the process earned the nickname the "Terrible Eight".

RIGHT: Scotland's iconic Grand Slam team of 1925. It would be Scotland's first ever Grand Slam, as they beat France 25-4, Wales 24-14, Ireland 14-8, and England 14-11 in front of 70,000 fans at Murrayfield.

–LEGENDS– Jack Kyle

Jack Kyle was named the greatest ever Irish rugby player in 2002. And although the Irish have produced many greats it's hard to argue with the Irish Rugby Board's decision.

Born in Belfast in 1926, Kyle went to Queen's University, Belfast, where he studied to become a doctor. It was at Queen's where he developed his love of rugby, playing for his university and then Ulster. He was a wonderful fly-half, having balance, bravery and skill, and that combination led to him gaining his first cap for Ireland in 1947 against France. Within the year he became a massive part of one of Ireland's greatest ever sides – the 1948/49 team who won the Grand Slam and Triple Crown. And it was Kyle who became the toast of the Irish public.

His performances for Ireland led to call-ups for the Barbarians and the British Lions; he was part of the latter's 1950 tour of New Zealand and Australia. Playing 19 games, including six test matches, Kyle played his last game for Ireland, against Scotland, in 1958. He had gained 46 caps for his beloved Ireland. After hanging up his boots he embarked on humanitarian work in Sumatra and Indonesia, and also worked as a consultant surgeon in Zambia. After returning from overseas, he set up the Jack Kyle Bursary at Queen's College, Belfast, in support of their Rugby Academy. In 2008 he was inducted into the International Rugby Board's Hall of Fame and was also given an OBE.

RIGHT: Jack Kyle (right) shakes hands with Cliff Morgan of Wales as the Irish arrive in Cardiff for the Five Nations.

BELOW: Jack Kyle in action in a game between Wales and Ireland. Jack kicks the ball forward, ready for another Irish attack.

RUGBY
–STATS–

Jack Kyle

Name: Jack Kyle

Born: Belfast 1926

Country: Ireland

Position: Fly-half

International Caps: 46

Clubs: Queen's College

Representative Honours: Ulster, British Lions, Barbarians

> "Jack Kyle was not only the best postwar fly half. But one of the all-time greats."
>
> Wallace Reyburn (writer)

The Fifties and Sixties

The start of the 1950s saw the demise of the great Ireland side and the emergence of the neighbours from across the channel, France, who, along with England and Wales, would dominate a fairly even decade in terms of the Five Nations. For Scotland and Ireland, the Fifties and Sixties would prove to be barren years, as the French and the Welsh took the Sixties by storm, both winning Grand Slams along the way.

The Wales Grand Slam team of 1952/53.

Led by skipper J A Gwilliam, an injury-ravaged Welsh team almost fell at the first hurdle in their 1952/53 campaign, just sneaking a 8-6 win over England at Twickenham. A 11-0 win at Arms Park over Scotland was followed by a 14-3 win in Ireland, while a 9-5 victory over France in Swansea made the Grand Slam secure.

The Irish rugby team of 1953 arriving at Cardiff airport before their Five Nations game with Wales. They finished third in the Championship, beating France and Scotland whilst drawing 9-9 with England.

ABOVE: The England team before the 1951 Home International game against Wales at Swansea. Wales won the game 23-5. England won only one game in the 1951 Championships – a 5-3 victory over Scotland at Twickenham.

LEFT: The England 1955 team pose for a photo before their Five Nations Championship campaign. It would be a poor year, as they finished fourth in the table, beating Scotland 9-6 and drawing 6-6 with Ireland.

LEFT: Ireland's 1955 team – which took the wooden spoon. They gained their only point against England in a 9-9 draw.

BELOW: The Wales team of 1955 pose for the camera before their match with Ireland. Wales shared the title with France, beating Ireland, England and the French along the way.

Wales versus Scotland in 1956. Wales centre Malcolm Thomas clears to touch under the gaze of team-mates Clem Thomas and W Williams. There was still straw on the pitch – groundsmen had placed it on the frozen ground so that the game at the Arms Park, Cardiff, could take place despite the treacherous conditions. Wales won the game 9-3.

LEFT: Scottish scrum-half Jat Rodd passes the ball out from a scrum during the Five Nations game between England and Scotland in 1958.

RIGHT: Wales captain Clem Thomas (left) gets to grips with French hooker Robert Vigier as the two teams clash at the Arms Park, Cardiff, in 1958. France won the game – it was their first in Wales for 50 years.

Ireland's 1959 Five Nations team before their game with Wales at the Arms Park.

Wales and England players leave the pitch at Cardiff after Wales win the 1959 international.

LEFT: Scotland's victorious new rugby captain, hooker Frank Laidlaw, is carried off the pitch by players and fans after the 14-5 win over England. Laidlaw played 32 times for Scotland and toured with the British Lions in 1966 and 1971. The former Scottish player Norman Mair once said of Laidlaw that "he considered the loss of a ball a family bereavement".

BELOW: Mud, mud, glorious mud. That's how it was in 1966 when Wales met Scotland in the Five Nations at Cardiff Arms Park.

Scotland skipper Jim Telfer (left) and Colin Blaikie (right) sign autographs for the fans at Abbotsinch airport on the team's return from Paris in 1969, where Scotland had defeated France 6-3.

The England rugby team training before the 1969 Five Nations. Led by captain Budge Rogers and newly appointed coach Don Whittle, England would beat France, Scotland and the South African tourists, although they also lost to Ireland and Wales in that year.

The Scotland forward line of 1965. Training (left to right) Ron Glasgow, Jim Telfer, Brian Neill, Norman Bruce, Peter Brown, David Rollo, Mike Campbell-Lamerton and Pringle Fisher.

The Team of the Decade:
The Seventies – 'Land Of My Fathers'

Throughout the world of rugby the Welsh team of the 1970s are rightly revered. The side have lived on not only in the memories of every Welshman but every rugby fan. They played with a style and panache that set them apart from every other side of that time. The team reads like a who's who of fabulous rugby players: Edwards, Bennett, J P R, Davies and John. After finishing with a Triple Crown in 1969, they dominated the next decade with three Grand Slams and one Triple Crown, and continued to evolve and get better as the years progressed. They set the benchmark for the way the game should be played.

One of the greatest teams ever – the Welsh 1976 side.

Left to right: Back row: John Bevan, Mike Knill, Graham Price, Trefor Evans, Allan Martin, Geoff Wheel, Charlie Faulkner, Bobby Windsor, Tommy David, Steve Fenwick, Roy Bergiers, Derek Quinnell, Roy Thomas. Front row: Brynmor Williams, Gerald Davies, J P R Williams, Gareth Edwards, Mervyn Davies, Phil Bennett, J J Williams, Ray Gravell.

Barry John and Gareth Edwards are carried off the Arms Park pitch by supporters after a Wales win against Ireland in 1971, which gave Wales the Triple Crown.

Two legends of the game, Barry John and Gareth Edwards, are presented with a pair of boots cast from their own at a ceremony in Cardiff.

Ray Gravell is showered with congratulations following his first try for Wales against Scotland at the Arms Park in 1978. Left to right: Charlie Faulkner, Phil Bennett, Ray Gravell, Terry Cobner, Gerald Davies, J P R Williams.

Scottish hooker Duncan Madsen is held by Bobby Windsor, as Windsor's team-mates Graham Price, Geoff Wheel and Allan Martin look on, in the 1977 Five Nations game.

Mervyn Davies with legendary headband.

Davies had many tough battles on the rugby pitch but his biggest was when he suffered a brain haemorrhage during a game for his club, Swansea, against Pontypool in 1976. Although told he would not play again, Davies recovered and went on to defy the doctors but retired soon after the surgery. As Wales captain he suffered only one defeat in nine games and will always be thought of as one of the game's great Number 8's.

–LEGENDS–

J P R Williams

John Peter Rhys Williams was born just outside Bridgend in 1949. When looking back at his distinguished career, it is clear that he must have been one of the game's great players – as he was known just by his initials, J P R.

Williams went to Bridgend Grammar School and then the prestigious Millfield School. It was at the latter that he developed into a great all-round sportsman. Not only did he excel in rugby but he won the Junior Wimbledon tournament in 1966, beating David Lloyd in the final. While pursuing a career in medicine, he turned his back on tennis in favour of rugby, and joined London Welsh Rugby Club, gaining his first international cap in a victory over Scotland at Murrayfield. Along with his devastating ability to kick the ball and run with it, he also had great skill as a tackler. Williams had it all and rugby fans of every nation knew it. J P R was part of the Wales team's golden era of the 1970s, and also represented the Barbarians and the British Lions. He hung up his international boots in 1981 to concentrate on his medical career, and retired fully in 2003. Williams was awarded the MBE for services to rugby and is now an orthopaedic surgeon. He was inducted into the Rugby Hall of Fame in 1997, an honour he thoroughly deserves.

J P R Williams passes the ball to namesake J J Williams as Wales play Scotland in 1976.

> "
> *I used to say I spent half my life breaking bones on the Rugby field, then the other half putting them back together in the operating room.*
>
> J P R Williams
> "

J P R in full flow, supported by Gerald Davies (left) and Jeff Young (right).

41

—LEGENDS—

Barry John

Although Barry John will always be referred to as "The King" his Wales career did not get off to the best of starts. Born in Cefneithin, Wales, in 1945, John joined his local team, where he played for two years before joining Llanelli Rugby Club. The young John showed that he was a special talent with the ability to unlock any defence and kick a ball with pinpoint precision, which, combined with a silky running style, made him destined for greatness. He made his international debut against Australia in 1966, ousting Welsh legend David Watkins from the side. But, after a 14-11 Australia win, John was dropped from the team and did not return until Watkins turned professional in 1967. Undeterred by this, the British Lions selectors picked him for the 1968 tour of South Africa, but John fractured his collarbone in the first test. On his return he guided Wales to the Triple Crown in 1969, and never looked back as he took the Welsh team to new heights, winning the first of many Grand Slams in 1971. John returned to the Lions as part of the New Zealand tour of 1971, where he established himself as one of the world's greatest fly-halves, particularly in the first test against the All Blacks, where his display was the talk of the tour. In total he scored 180 points in New Zealand, and he returned as "The King". A year later, aged 27, John announced his retirement from the game. It was a bombshell that shook not only Welsh rugby but the game as a whole. John played his last game for Wales in the 20-6 victory over France, ensuring that "The King" went out at the top.

Barry John, with support from Dai Morris and Mervyn Davies, makes a break for goal in the match with England in 1970.

An injured Barry John is carried off the pitch by wing-forwards Omri Jones (left) and Ken Braddock, after gashing his leg in a Wales trial match.

RUGBY
–STATS–

Barry John

Name: Barry John

Born: Cefneithin 1945

Country: Wales

Position: Fly-half

International Caps: 25

Clubs: Llanelli, Cardiff

Representative Honours: British Lions, Barbarians

" *His kicking was phenomenal – he could put a ball on a sixpence.* "

Rodney Webb (England 1967–1972)

43

–LEGENDS–

Phil Bennett

Phil Bennett will always be remembered for the jinking sidesteps that wrong-footed three All Blacks in the Barbarians' game of 1973. The move led to the try by countryman Gareth Edwards that has been referred to as the "greatest try ever". The little man from Llanelli made his debut for Wales in 1969 against France in Paris, when he came on for Gerald Davies. As Barry John was in the fly-half seat, Bennett spent his time being shuffled from wing to centre to full-back. It was not until John's shock retirement that Bennett found his spiritual home at fly-half. Unfazed by taking over John's mantle, Bennett came alive and showed the rugby public just what he could do with his jinking runs, feints and tricks. He was fantastic on the British Lions tour of South Africa in 1974, scoring 103 points along the way. Bennett became Wales captain in 1977, and also became only the second Welshman to skipper the Lions on their 1977 tour of New Zealand. Many felt his game suffered with the responsibility of the captaincy on the tour, as the Lions lost 3-1. But Bennett bounced back to lead the Welsh team to another Triple Crown that same year, as well as the Grand Slam in 1978. Bennett retired later that year and was inducted into the Rugby Hall of Fame in 2007.

RIGHT: Phil Bennett in action for Wales in their 18-9 victory against Scotland in Cardiff, 1970.

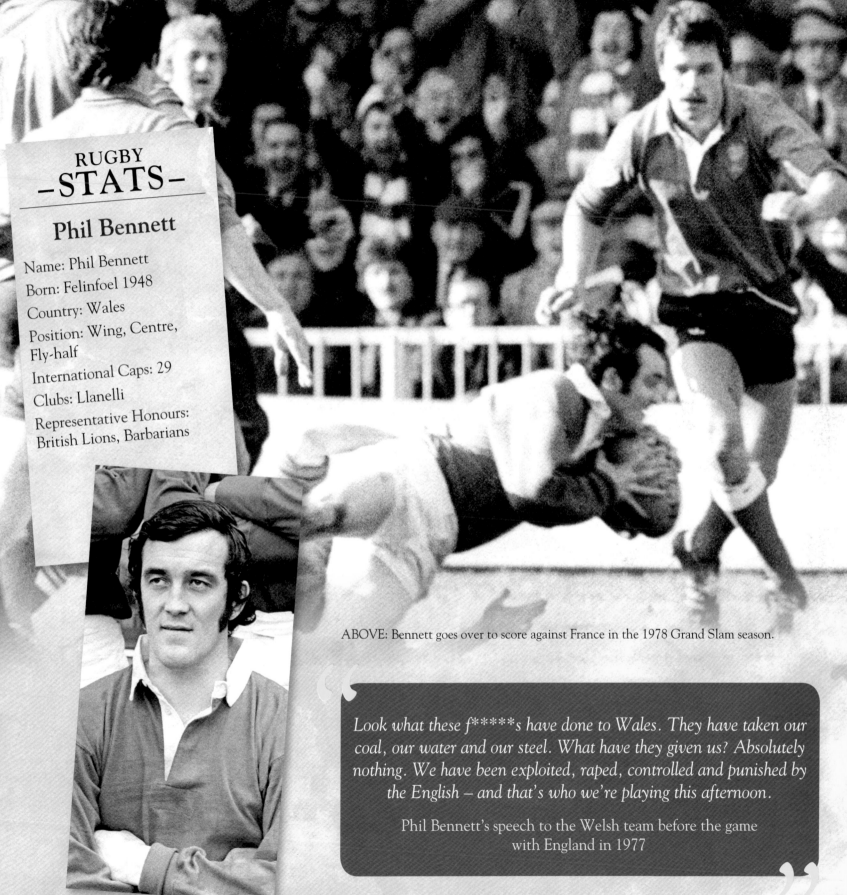

RUGBY
–STATS–

Phil Bennett

Name: Phil Bennett

Born: Felinfoel 1948

Country: Wales

Position: Wing, Centre, Fly-half

International Caps: 29

Clubs: Llanelli

Representative Honours: British Lions, Barbarians

ABOVE: Bennett goes over to score against France in the 1978 Grand Slam season.

> Look what these f*****s have done to Wales. They have taken our coal, our water and our steel. What have they given us? Absolutely nothing. We have been exploited, raped, controlled and punished by the English – and that's who we're playing this afternoon.
>
> Phil Bennett's speech to the Welsh team before the game with England in 1977

45

–LEGENDS–

Gerald Davies

Gerald Davies was the beating heart of the great Welsh team of the 1970s. From 1968 to 1978 he baffled and bewildered opposing players with his dazzling footwork. Many feel he was at his best on the 1971 Lions tour of New Zealand, where he ran in three tries during the test series. He was born in Llantrisant in 1945 and trained as a schoolteacher. He gained his first international cap in 1966 as a centre, and he made such an impact in the Wales team that he was chosen for the 1968 Lions tour of South Africa. Although dogged by injury on the tour, he repaid the faith shown in him with a dazzling display in the third test against the Springboks.

With speed a big part of his game, he switched to wing three-quarter in 1969 and became even more deadly. After Grand Slam success with Wales he returned to the Lions in 1971 and went on their tour of New Zealand. There, he showed the world how great he was. He retired in 1978 and became a journalist, writing for *The Times*. His youth work in Wales earned him a CBE in the 2002 honours list, and, in 2007, it was announced he would be the manager of the 2009 British and Irish Lions tour of South Africa. Unfortunately, the Lions were defeated 2-1 in the test series.

RIGHT: Gerald Davies touches down for his second try against England in the 1971 Five Nations.

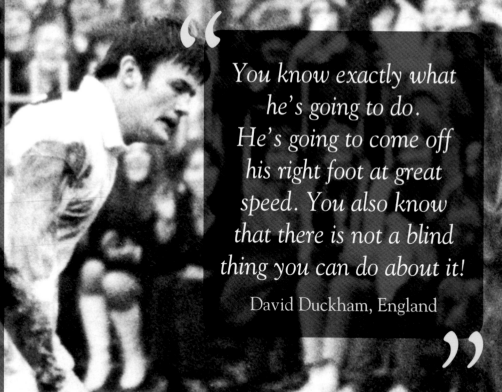

> *You know exactly what he's going to do. He's going to come off his right foot at great speed. You also know that there is not a blind thing you can do about it!*
>
> David Duckham, England

RUGBY –STATS–

Gerald Davies

Name: Gerald Davies

Born: Llantrisant 1945

Country: Wales

Position: Centre, Wing

International Caps: 46

Clubs: Cambridge University, Cardiff, London Welsh

Representative Honours: British Lions, Barbarians

Gerald Davies in action against Scotland in the Five Nations.

The Eighties and Nineties

The 1980s started with an England Grand Slam – and that's as good as it got for the men in white all decade. Wales shared the Triple Crown with France towards the end of the decade, and with that being the Welshmen's only success it would confirm the struggle they were about to endure to repeat past glories. The decade was dominated by the French, with the Scots providing a surprise Grand Slam in 1984, and the Irish also enjoying some success, with two Triple Crowns in 1982 and 1985. The 1990s started with the dominance of England, as Will Carling led them to back-to-back Grand Slams early in the decade. For Ireland and Wales the 1990s would see another decade of struggle, but, for the Scots, the end of the 1990s would see them achieve a Championship at last.

Scotland's rugby heroes of 1984, looking pleased with themselves at a celebration to mark the first Grand Slam by the Scots since 1925.

England rugby captains through the years meet up for a photo opportunity in 1980. Left to right, back: Dickie Jeeps, Budge Rogers, John Pullin and Jeff Butterfield. Front: Roger Uttley, Bill Beaumont, John Kendall-Carpenter and Ron Jacobs.

England and Bath prop Gareth Chilcott (Number 3) and Dean Richards (Number 8) have an altercation with some of the Welsh team during the Wales versus England Five Nations game at Cardiff Arms Park.

England and Ireland battle it out at Twickenham in 1992. England won the game 38-9, and went on to win the Five Nations that year, while the Irish won it the following year.

–LEGENDS–

Will Carling

It is safe to say that Will Carling did not enjoy the greatest of relationships with the RFU or the press during his time as England captain. But events and tabloid stories about his private life must not mask the fact he pulled English rugby through a very dark tunnel in the late 1980s and into the light of success, capped by Grand Slams and Triple Crowns in the early 1990s.

Carling was born in Bradford-on-Avon in 1965, and had a taste of things to come when he captained England Schoolboys as an 18-year-old. He joined Harlequins, and represented the Barbarians before his 22nd birthday. Asked by England coach Geoff Cooke to lead the team out against Australia at Twickenham in place of Bristol's Richard Harding, Carling took to the responsibility like a duck to water. It was a bold move by Cooke but it paid off, as England won 28-19. A formidable partnership between captain and coach was born. It was not, however, all plain sailing for Carling, as he missed the 1989 Lions tour through injury and then had the humiliation of seeing outsiders Scotland beat an overconfident England to the Grand Slam in 1990. This was quickly forgotten a year later when Carling led England to their first Grand Slam for 11 years, and to the final of the World Cup, where they lost 12-6 to Australia. In 1992 he took England to a further Grand Slam victory, repeating the feat in 1995. After the 1995 success Carling told a TV reporter that the RFU Committee were, "A bunch of old farts." This led to his sacking as captain but, following a public apology, he was reinstated. After a disastrous World Cup campaign by England in 1995, Carling took the anger of the press on his shoulders, stepping down from the captaincy in 1996 after England had won the Triple Crown. Carling continued to play for England but retired after their 34-13 win against Wales in Cardiff, which gave England another Triple Crown. After his career ended Carling carved out a living as a TV pundit. After all, he was never shy in giving an opinion.

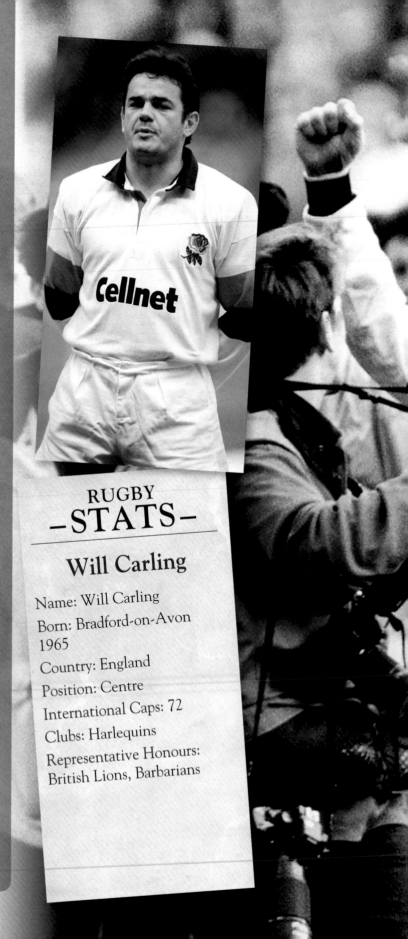

RUGBY –STATS–

Will Carling

Name: Will Carling

Born: Bradford-on-Avon 1965

Country: England

Position: Centre

International Caps: 72

Clubs: Harlequins

Representative Honours: British Lions, Barbarians

England captain Will Carling celebrates the win over Scotland, 1995.

ABOVE: Will Carling in reflective mood for England.

RIGHT: Will Carling, England's captain, running with the ball in the Five Nations game against Ireland, 1991.

Scotland celebrate beating England in the 1983 Calcutta Cup game at Twickenham. The Calcutta Cup was presented to the Rugby Football Union in 1878 by the Calcutta Rugby Club. They had joined the RFU in 1874 with a view to playing matches, but they disbanded due to a lack of members. The club withdrew their money from the bank, which was in silver rupees, and had it melted down to make the trophy that England and Scotland play for today.

–LEGENDS–

Scotland's Gavin Hastings kicking a ball placed by the team-mate lying on the pitch.

Gavin Hastings

Gavin Hastings was a man brought up on rivalries. How could he not be, coming from a family with three brothers? Hastings started his career at school, and became the first player to captain a Scottish Schoolboy team that won in England. In 1985 he also captained Cambridge University as they beat Oxford in the varsity match at Twickenham. A natural successor to the great Andy Irvine as full-back for Scotland, Hastings got his chance against France in 1986, along with his brother Scott, as Scotland won a tight game 18-17.

After representing Scotland in the 1987 World Cup, Hastings was selected as first-choice full-back for the Lions tour of Australia in 1989. This was the tour that announced Hastings to the world: he scored a personal total of 66 points as the Lions beat Australia over three tests. After the success of the tour, Hastings cemented his place in the hearts of all Scottish rugby fans when he was part of the 1990 Grand Slam side and, a year later, when he helped the Scots to a semi-final place in the World Cup. In 1993 he was given the honour of captaining the British Lions tour of New Zealand, where the Lions went down 2-1. On his return, Hastings captained Scotland and, although they were a struggling side, he continued to be the "best full-back in the world". After retiring in 1996 he was inducted into the Rugby Hall of Fame in 2003. He is now involved in various charity works and with TV punditry.

Hastings in full flow against England.

> *Gavin is a big man in every sense of the word. His greatest asset was to engender confidence in those around him and to lead by example when the opposition had to be taken on. In New Zealand they considered him simply the best full-back in the world.*
>
> Sir Ian McGeechan, former national coach of Scotland and the British Lions

RUGBY
–STATS–

Gavin Hastings

Name: Gavin Hastings

Born: Edinburgh 1962

Country: Scotland

Position: Full-back

International Caps: 61

Clubs: Cambridge University, London Scottish, Watsonians

Representative Honours: British Lions, Barbarians

The Hastings brothers, Gavin and Scott, holding hard hats at the newly developed Murrayfield Stadium.

–LEGENDS–

Jeremy Guscott

When Jeremy Guscott went through the gears it was like watching a Formula One car. His running from behind the scrum was a thing to behold. Guscott had an air of arrogance about him that may have meant many TV interviewers did not warm to him, but on the pitch he had it all. Born in Bath in 1965, Guscott was an extraordinary talent. He was not your university-educated player like many of his generation; in fact, he was a bricklayer and then worked for British Gas in the very last days of the amateur scene. Guscott marked his England debut against Romania with a hat-trick of tries, and made such an impact in the game that he was chosen to tour Australia with the British Lions – where he promptly scored on his debut, becoming the first man since Jeff Butterfield in 1955 to score on both his England and Lions debuts. Due to his devastating partnership with Will Carling, he won Grand Slam after Grand Slam with a wonderful England side in the 1990s, and in 1997, on the British Lions tour of South Africa, he landed a fantastic drop goal to win the match and the series. At home he helped Bath dominate the 1990s with a string of league titles and Pilkington Cups. Guscott retired in 1999, and in 2000 he was awarded the MBE for services to rugby.

Guscott in full flow for England against Italy in the World Cup.

Guscott in action in the Calcutta Cup against Scotland.

RUGBY -STATS-

Jeremy Guscott

Name: Jeremy Guscott
Born: Bath 1965
Country: England
Position: Centre
International Caps: 65
Clubs: Bath
Representative Honours: British Lions, Barbarians

"

Jerry Guscott has been an invaluable support to younger players and an England centre to remember. He epitomised the best in English rugby.

Clive Woodward, ex-England and Lions coach

"

Scotland's Stuart Grimes wins the line-out against England in Scotland's 24-21 defeat at Twickenham. Grimes played 71 times for Scotland, making his debut against Australia in 1997.

Welsh winger Nigel Walker on his way to a try, pursued by the French, in Wales' 24-15 victory in 1994. Walker represented Great Britain in the 1984 Olympics in the 110-metre hurdles. He switched sports to play for his home town club, Cardiff, and gained 17 caps for Wales.

Brothers in arms. Tony (left) and Rory (right) Underwood pose for the cameras before the start of England's test match against South Africa. Tony played for Leicester Tigers and Newcastle Falcons, and gained 27 caps for England as well as a call-up for the British Lions. Today he is a long-haul pilot for Virgin Airways. He lives on the Swiss–French border with his wife and children. Rory also played for Leicester Tigers; he gained 85 caps for England as well as six for the British Lions. He also played for the Barbarians. He left the RAF in 1999 and today runs a management company. The Underwoods were the first brothers to play for England since Arthur and Harold Wheatley played together against Scotland in 1937.

Ireland's Paddy Johns is halted by Gareth Thomas of Wales in the Five Nations.

England's Richard Hill does battle with Scotland's Kenny Logan.

England's Brian Moore lashes out at Scotland's Craig Chalmers as team-mates try to keep them apart during the Five Nations game in 1995. England went on to win 24-12 and take the Grand Slam.

Scotland's Alan Tait celebrates a Scottish try. Tait won 27 caps for Scotland as well as playing twice for the British Lions. He played for Newcastle and also switched codes in his career, turning out for Widnes and Leeds.

Wales' Ieuan Evans. Evans will always be held in high regard by the Welsh fans. He gained 72 caps for Wales and scored 157 points, making him the third highest try scorer for his country. He also played seven times for the Lions, as well as for the Barbarians, and played club rugby at Llanelli and Bath. In 1996 he was awarded the MBE for services to rugby.

Welsh wonder Ieuan Evans pictured with the Five
Nations trophy after Wales won the 1994 Championship.

RUGBY
–STATS–

Keith Wood

Name: Keith Wood

Born: Killaloe 1972

Country: Ireland

Position: Hooker

International Caps: 58

Clubs: Garryowen, Harlequins, Munster

Representative Honours: British Lions

Keith Wood

If ever a player put his heart and soul into the game it was Keith Wood. Wood was born in Killaloe in Ireland in 1972, and played for Garryowen, where he helped them to the All-Ireland title in 1992 and 1994. He left for Harlequins in 1995, the year after he made his Ireland debut against Australia. Wood always put his body on the line, and it was this attitude that made him a favourite with the Ireland fans as well as the British Lions selectors, who chose him for the 1997 and 2001 Lions tours. His greatest strength, along with his bullish tackling, was leadership in open play, and he dominated the world's number one hooker spot. Wood returned to Ireland to play for Munster in 1999 but he only stayed for one season. In 2001 he was named World Player of the Year; he retired from the game in 2003. His contribution to rugby was recognized in 2005 when he was inducted into the Rugby Hall of Fame. Today he works for the BBC and the *Daily Telegraph* as a freelance journalist.

Wood scores a try against England at Lansdowne Road.

England's Grand Slammers: 'Swing Low Sweet Chariot'

The England side of the early 1990s were a phenomenal team. They won three Grand Slams in 1991, 1992 and 1995, as well as two Triple Crowns in 1996 and 1997.

England captain Will Carling celebrates with "The boys of 1992", after beating Wales 24-0 to win the Grand Slam at Twickenham.

The Underwood brothers, Tony and Rory, pose with team-mate Rob Andrew before a game at Twickenham in the 1992 Grand Slam year. Their contribution to the Grand Slam side of the early 1990s was huge.

A formidable Grand Slam front row of (left to right) Jeff Probyn, Brian Moore and Jason Leonard. Head down and ready to go.

Rory Underwood goes for the line as England play Wales at Cardiff Arms Park.

81

The LIONS

The 1977 Lions squad before their tour of New Zealand.

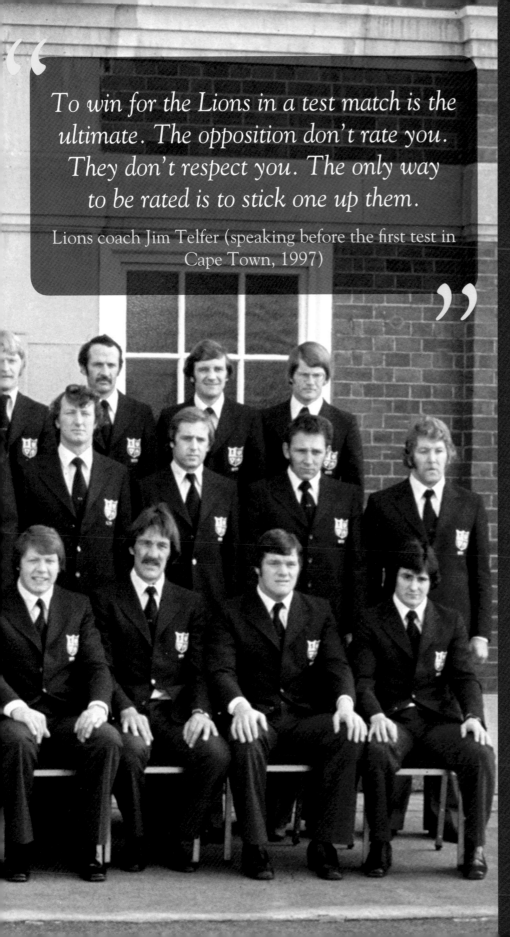

> "To win for the Lions in a test match is the ultimate. The opposition don't rate you. They don't respect you. The only way to be rated is to stick one up them."
>
> Lions coach Jim Telfer (speaking before the first test in Cape Town, 1997)

When a rugby player hangs up his boots at the end of a career there can be no more satisfying thought than "I was an international. But I was also a Lion." The British and Irish Lions epitomize everything this great game is about: standing toe-to-toe with your team-mates ready to play for your country, knowing that you are the best the nation has to offer and that the hopes of England, Scotland, Ireland and Welsh fans rest with you.

Many have worn the shirt with pride over the decades as they go to tackle the southern hemisphere's best in the shape of New Zealand, Australia and South Africa. The first official tour as the British Isles was in 1910 to South Africa, and every three years since a team made from the Home Nations has picked a squad to do battle overseas. There have been many highlights over the years: the Lions team of 1971, who lost only one game on the tour to New Zealand, and the 1974 team led by Irishman Willie John McBride, who went to South Africa and came back unbeaten in 22 games. The Lions tour means just as much to modern players as it did to those in the past, and there can be no greater accolade for rugby players than to say "I was a Lion."

1888 First unofficial tour of the southern hemisphere. **1910** The first official tour to South Africa. The team are known as the British Isles. **1924** British Isles, now referred to as the Lions, lose all four tests in South Africa. **1927** Lions tour Argentina. **1930** Combined tour of New Zealand and Australia (the Lions wear red tops instead of blue). **1938** Tour of South Africa. **1950** After a 12-year break the team tour New Zealand and Australia. **1956** Lions draw series in South Africa 2-2. **1959** Lions lose six out of 35 matches in New Zealand and Australia. **1962** South Africa win three out of the four tests against the Lions. **1966** John Robins becomes the Lions' first coach and takes them to New Zealand. Lions beat Canada in Toronto, on the way home from the New Zealand tour. **1971** A legendary side lose only one game in New Zealand. **1974** Willie John McBride leads the team to an unbeaten 22 games in South Africa. **1977** Lions lose test 3-1 in New Zealand. **1980** Lions lose three tests in South Africa. **1983** All Blacks whitewash Lions 3-0 in test series. **1989** New coach Ian McGeechan leads team to win the series 2-1 in Australia. **1993** McGeechan's team lose 2-1 in New Zealand test series. **1997** England's Martin Johnson leads the Lions to a 2-1 win in South Africa. **2001** British Lions become the British and Irish Lions and lose series in Australia. **2005** Lions lose series 3-0 in New Zealand. **2009** Defeat in South Africa 2-1 in the test series. **2013** Warren Gatland announced as coach to take a Lions team to Australia.

RIGHT: The iconic Lions badge depicted the four Home Nations.

Davies of Harlequins and England scores against Orange Free State on the 1955 tour of South Africa. The 1955 tour was captained by Robert Thompson and coached by Jack Siggins, both of Ireland. The Lions played 25 games and won 19, lost five and drew one. They also tied the series with the Springboks 2-2.

ABOVE: The British Lions tour of South Africa in 1955.
Players celebrate their victory with a song.

RIGHT: The 1968 tour team leaving for South Africa.
The Lions were led in 1968 by Tom Kiernan of Ireland;
however, the tour was a disappointment as they lost 3-0 to
the Springboks.

—LEGENDS—

Cliff Morgan

Cliff Morgan was the conductor to the symphony that was the 1955 British Lions. His fantastic balance, strength and acceleration drove one of the greatest back lines any team could possess. With Jeff Butterfield and Arthur Smith, and Cecil Pedlow and Tony O'Reilly out on the wings, they emerged on the 1955 tour of South Africa as world stars.

Born in Trebanog, Wales, in 1930, Morgan joined Cardiff Rugby Club straight from school. After being picked for the Barbarians in 1950, he was quickly called up for his international debut for Wales against Ireland in 1951. Morgan never forgot the emotion of the day, particularly as he was opposite his own hero – Ireland's legendary Jack Kyle. Morgan became a major part of the Wales team, winning the Grand Slam in 1952 and then being made captain of his country in 1956. His reputation was stamped for all to see on the 1955 Lions tour to South Africa. The first test game against the Springboks is argued to be the "greatest game ever", as Morgan brought the Lions level with only 14 men after Reg Higgins' injury. The Lions eventually won the game 23-22 in front of a crowd of 100,000. Morgan showed on the tour what an inspiration he was, as he was christened by the local papers "Morgan the Magnificent". Cliff Morgan retired from the game in 1958, with his last game being for the Barbarians against East Africa in Nairobi. On retirement he found a new career in broadcasting, making his own little bit of history with his legendary commentary of Gareth Edwards' famous try for the Barbarians against the All Blacks in 1973. Morgan was given the OBE for services to broadcasting and inducted into the Rugby Hall of Fame in 2009. His passionate commentary matched the way he played the game, and he will always be remembered as one of the greats.

Sportsmen of different eras. Cliff Morgan (centre) chats to football's Kevin Keegan (left) and Sir Bobby Charlton (right).

Cliff Morgan of Wales kicks the ball into touch in the 1956 Five Nations game against France.

RUGBY
-STATS-

Cliff Morgan

Name: Cliff Morgan

Born: Trebanog 1930

Country: Wales

Position: Fly-half

International Caps: 29

Clubs: Cardiff

Representative Honours:
British Lions, Barbarians

–LEGENDS–

Willie John McBride

William James McBride is a man with an almost mythical reputation. Born in Toombridge, Northern Ireland, Willie John, as he was known, did not start playing rugby until he was 17 years old. He was a man mountain – standing at 6ft 3in tall and weighing in at 17 stone he was a no-nonsense player and anybody who stood in his way knew it. But, above all, he had the sort of qualities that would make other team-mates run through a brick wall to follow him. That was never more evident than when he led the British Lions in South Africa in 1974. The Springboks had a fiercesome reputation for the physical side of the game, and McBride took the attitude that the Lions would fight fire with fire and not be intimidated. It was a philosophy that worked, as the Lions won 21 games out of 22, and it ensured McBride gained legendary status with every rugby fan.

McBride started his career with Ulster, and his build made him a natural as a forward. He then moved on to Ballymena, and later made his debut for Ireland in 1962 against England at Twickenham, with England running out 16-0 winners. McBride was chosen for the 1962 Lions tour of South Africa but, on that occasion, the Lions came home defeated. The 1966 Lions tour of New Zealand made its mark on McBride, and even more on his opposite number, Colin Meads. Meads alleged the punch he received from McBride in one of the tests was the hardest he had ever had inflicted on him. After that the two had a mutual respect for each other. McBride took part in a record five Lions tours, and the Lions have never had such an inspirational captain. He played his last game for Ireland in 1975 against France, and caused a near riot as he scored his one and only try in the match. He later managed the 1983 Lions tour of New Zealand and, in 1997, he was inducted into the Rugby Hall of Fame. Willie John will always be regarded as the "Ultimate Lion".

Willie John McBride, Ireland and British Lions legendary captain, in 1971.

RUGBY
–STATS–

Willie John McBride

Name: Willie John McBride

Born: Toombridge 1940

Country: Ireland

Position: Lock

International Caps: 63

Clubs: Ballymena

Representative Honours: Ulster, British Lions, Barbarians

Willie John reunited with his family after the Lions victory in South Africa.

Willie John McBride was a fierce leader of the Lions. In the build-up to the tour the Springboks had let everyone know that they would intimidate the Lions. McBride decided on "getting in first" so he instigated the famous "99 call", which meant when it was called the whole of the side would "stick it" to the Springboks. The plan did little for the reputation of the game but certainly secured the Lions' dominance on the tour.

Action from the 1971 third test at Athletic Park, Wellington, New Zealand. The Lions won the test 13-3, with tries from Gerald Davies and Barry John.

Action from Eden Park, Auckland, New Zealand. This was the fourth test game, with the Lions winning the series 2-1. A draw or victory for the Lions would have given them the overall series. With the game poised at 11-11, Lions full-back J P R Williams received the ball 45 metres out and attempted a drop goal, which he converted to put the Lions 14-11 ahead. It was the only drop goal Williams ever landed in his test career. New Zealand fought back to draw the game but the result still gave the Lions the overall test victory.

Lions captain John Dawes and All Blacks captain Colin Meads lead out their respective teams at Carisbrook, Dunedin, New Zealand, in 1971. The Lions won the game.

Captain Willie John McBride (waving) salutes the crowd at Heathrow airport as the victorious Lions return from the 1974 tour of South Africa. The Lions won the series 3-0; they were the first Lions team to win in South Africa.

Lions fans welcome them home to Heathrow after the 1974 tour of South Africa, during which they won the series 3-0.

Captain Phil Bennett, complete with Lions mascot, leads the team before they fly out to New Zealand for the 1977 tour.

BELOW: Prince Charles shares a joke with England and Lions forward Bill Beaumont before the Lions 1977 game with the Barbarians. Beaumont played 34 times for England and seven times for the Lions. He also captained the Lions on the 1980 tour of Australia, becoming the first Englishman to captain the Lions since Doug Prentice in 1930. In 2008 Beaumont was awarded the OBE for services to rugby.

A very strange
advertising photo for
the British Lions 1977
tour. Left to right:
Allan Martin, Willie
Duggan, Morris Keen,
Nigel Horton and
Gordon Brown.

The British Lions arrive home from South Africa in 1997, after winning the series. The tour was the first after apartheid had been abolished in the country, and, with South Africa as world champions in 1995, the Lions were the underdogs. But, led by Martin Johnson, they won the series 2-1.

Phil Bennett, the Lions captain for the 1977 tour of New Zealand, with mascot, before leaving Heathrow airport.

–LEGENDS–

Mike Gibson

Looking at him, many felt that Mike Gibson would never be a rugby player. But if ever looks were deceptive that was the case with Gibson. Although slight in appearance, he was crunching in the tackle. And as for being tackled, many could not get near this swift Irishman. His qualities of determination and courage, along with a wonderful turn of speed, led him to a record number of test caps for Ireland and also had some people suggesting he was the best all-round back in the world.

Gibson was born in Belfast in 1942, and played for Cambridge University while training to be a solicitor. He made his Ireland debut in 1964, playing at fly-half in Ireland's 18-5 win over England at Twickenham, their first success at the ground for 16 years. Gibson was picked for the 1966 Lions tour to New Zealand and the 1968 tour to South Africa, and he used those tours as much-needed experience. Like many of his contemporaries, Gibson's finest hour came on the 1971 tour of New Zealand, when he formed the perfect midfield trio with Wales pair Barry John and John Dawes – the New Zealand public loved Gibson's attacking flair and style. He was picked for the 1974 tour of South Africa, but due to work commitments he could only join it as a replacement. A man of records, Gibson played on five Lions tours and 69 times for Ireland: his final appearance in the green shirt was against Australia in 1979, which, at 36 years of age, made him the oldest Irish man to win a cap.

Irish fly-half Gibson kicks for goal against England.

Gibson in full flow for Ireland against England in 1972.

BELOW: Mike Gibson (centre) with fellow British Lions Wales player J J Williams (left), and Scotland's Ian McGeechan (right), at the International Sports Writers' Club in London before the 1977 Lions tour of New Zealand.

–LEGENDS–

Finlay Calder

Finlay Calder holds a unique place in British Lions history, as he is the only 20th-century captain to lead the team to a series victory after losing the opening test. Calder was born in Haddington, Scotland, in 1957. He made his Scotland debut in 1986 against France. And, after some determined displays for his country, he was picked to captain the British Lions on the 1989 tour of Australia. His drive and determination overcame the shortcomings many critics felt he had at the time. He was also following his twin brother Jim, who was a Lion in 1983; the Calder brothers became the first twins to ever play for the British Lions. The 1989 tour was Finlay Calder's finest hour: after losing the first test he rallied his troops in the face of some fierce criticism from the Australian press, who alleged the Lions were too physical. Calder showed he was a mountain of a man off the pitch as well as on it by taking – along with coach Ian McGeechan – all the flak, and shielding his team-mates. They all repaid the support by winning the series 2-1, and coming home victorious. Calder retired in 1991, playing his last game for Scotland against Wales. He will always be remembered in Lions history as a true captain and leader of men.

Finlay Calder

Name: Finlay Calder

Born: Haddington 1957

Country: Scotland

Position: Flanker

International Caps: 34

Clubs: Stewart's Melville FP, Heriot's FP

Representative Honours: British Lions

Finlay Calder here in action for his native Scotland.

–LEGENDS–

Mike Burton

Mike Burton was the typical one-club man. He also had an uncompromising determination to succeed at this great sport of rugby. Born in Maidenhead in 1945, Burton made his debut for his beloved Gloucester in 1964 at the age of 18. He went on to make 360 appearances for the club, and led them to success in the John Player Cup in 1972 and 1978. He made his England debut in 1972 at Twickenham against Wales. Burton continued to be a cornerstone of the English side, and was a member of the victorious England team that toured South Africa in 1972 and came home undefeated.

He toured again in 1973 to New Zealand, and was also a member of the famous 1974 British Lions team that again were invincible in South Africa. Never a shrinking violet, Burton gave everything for the shirt and crossed many a referee, particularly on England's 1975 tour of Australia – where he became the first Englishman to be sent off at international level. Burton played 17 times for England, a number that would have been at least doubled, if not for some strange team selections by the RFU at the time. He also represented the Barbarians. He is truly somebody who has evolved with the game he loved. After retiring from the sport, Burton went into the sports marketing business with great success, and his Mike Burton Group has now been the leading light in global sports marketing for over 30 years. Mike is also involved with the Barbarians where he has been on the committee since 2005.

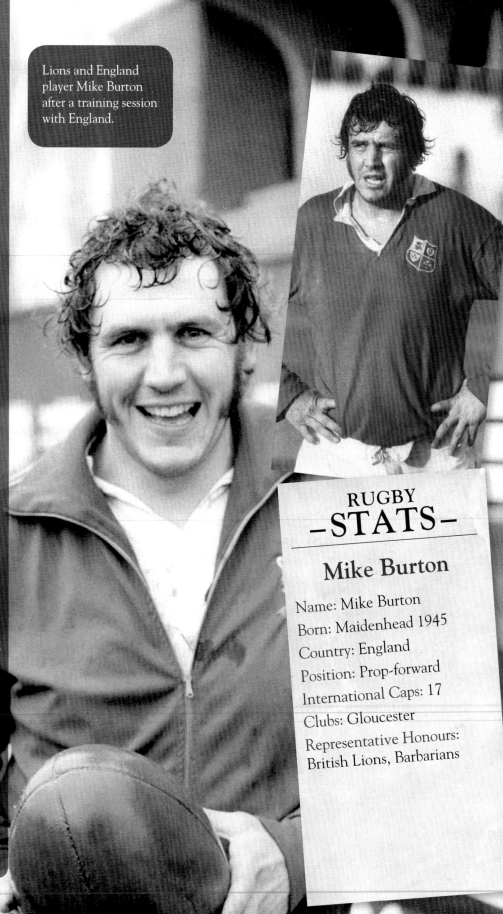

Lions and England player Mike Burton after a training session with England.

RUGBY –STATS–

Mike Burton

Name: Mike Burton

Born: Maidenhead 1945

Country: England

Position: Prop-forward

International Caps: 17

Clubs: Gloucester

Representative Honours: British Lions, Barbarians

Mike Burton relaxing at home with his wife Pat and their children.

ABOVE: Mike Burton and the British Lions pose for a photo before kick-off against South Africa. Left to right: Jeff Evans, Mervyn Davies, Mike Burton, Bobby Windsor.

LEFT: The Lions relaxing on the beach in South Africa during the 1974 tour. Left to right: Gordon Brown, Phil Bennett, Bobby Windsor, Mike Burton, Gareth Edwards, Fergus Slattery, J J Williams, J P R Williams.

The Coaches

Legendary Lions coach Carwyn Jones being interviewed in 1972. Jones was truly ahead of his time. Born in 1929 and the son of a coal miner, he played fly-half for Llanelli and Wales, and he would have got more than the two caps he gained if he had not been up against a certain Cliff Morgan for the role. After spells as a player at Llanelli and London Welsh, he became the Lions coach on the famous 1971 tour of New Zealand – and with his style of quiet words rather than shouted orders, along with a passion for attacking rugby, the victory over New Zealand will be remembered forever. On his return he joined Llanelli as coach and masterminded the side's famous victory over the All Blacks in 1972, again showing his legendary status as a coach. Carwyn died, of natural causes, in 1983 in a hotel room in Amsterdam.

Lions 1997 coach Fran Cotton. Cotton is truly a larger-than-life character on and off the field. As a player he captained England on three occasions during the dark days of the 1970s. He represented the Lions on the 1974 and 1977 tests, had to return early from the 1980 tour with chest pains, then was asked to coach them again in 1997. After rugby, Cotton, along with England team-mate Steve Smith, set up Cotton Traders, supplying leisure clothing.

ABOVE: Fran, in his playing days, laying down the law to his team-mates at an England training session.

ABOVE: Jim Telfer. Martin Johnson said of this tough Scot, "He could make grown men cry after one of his training sessions." Like his coaching partner and countryman Ian McGeechan, Jim Telfer's contribution to the Lions came from both sides of the touchline. Telfer toured with the Lions in 1966 and 1968, where his forthright style as captain earned the respect of team-mates and opponents. He also coached the Lions in 1983, and became the forwards coach under McGeechan in 1997, seeing the successful 2-1 series win in South Africa.

RIGHT: Lions 2005 coach Clive Woodward (middle) shares a joke with captain Michael Owen (right) and vice-captain Jonny Wilkinson (left) in May 2005.

Woodward played for England 21 times and was also on the 1980 Lions tour of South Africa and the 1983 tour of New Zealand. He became coach of England in 1997 until 2004. During this time, he oversaw one of the greatest times in English rugby, which culminated in the winning of the World Cup in 2003 – an honour that led to Woodward becoming a Knight of the Realm in the Queen's honours list. He coached the British and Irish Lions on the 2005 tour of New Zealand, but the tourists were beaten 3-0 in the series. Always interested in various sports, Woodward has since become involved in Southampton Football Club and the British Olympic Association.

New 2013 coach, New Zealander Warren Gatland. Gatland played 17 times for his native New Zealand before embarking on a successful coaching career. He joined London Wasps in 2002 and oversaw three domestic titles and a Heineken Cup win. He returned to New Zealand but was tempted back with the offer to turn Wales around; in his first game in control they beat England 26-19, after trailing 19-6 with nearly 60 minutes played. To date he has led the Welsh to Grand Slams and Triple Crowns as well as to a World Cup semi-final in 2011. He will lead the 2013 British and Irish Lions in Australia, and with his credentials it could very well be a successful tour.

When
RUGBY Was **RUGBY**

Rivals Across the Sea
"THE TOURISTS"

Jonah Lomu of New Zealand leads the 'haka' prior to the tourists' game against England in 1999. The haka is an ancestral war cry from the Maori people of New Zealand, and the All Blacks first started to use the chant in 1905. There are many different types of haka, but the All Blacks favour the 'Ka Mate' chant.

> *In war you can be outnumbered but in rugby you are man for man.*
>
> Paul Roos, South Africa captain 1906

There can be no finer test for any national rugby team than to defend their country against a visiting team from overseas. The scenario is the closest thing we can get to a bloodless war, although sometimes it is not entirely bloodless!

Over the years many wonderful teams have arrived on the UK shores to take on the might of this great nation. In 1905 the very first visitors to this country were the fantastic New Zealand side. It was this tour that led the British press to name the side the "All Blacks". The tour cost the New Zealand Rugby Football Union £5,000 to put on, and it took the team three months to get to our shores, but it was worth waiting for as they beat England 15-0 in front of 80,000 people at the Oval in London. This wetted the rugby fraternity's appetite, and tours by other countries followed.

Some of the tours have not been a complete success; for instance, the 1936 Australian team arrived in this country only to find out that the Second World War had broken out and they had to return without putting their boots on. And, in 1969, the South African tourists saw their tour littered with anti-apartheid demonstrations – with a bit of rugby thrown in for good measure. The touring system is still part of rugby, with teams from all over the world coming to these islands to test themselves. Unfortunately, today's tours usually feature games against the Home Nations only, whereas years ago the games would include matches against local clubs. Who will ever forget Welsh club Newport's victory over the All Blacks in 1963, and Llanelli's win against a legendary All Blacks team in 1972. It's a tradition in the game that must never be lost, as it opens up these shores to the world.

1905 First ever New Zealand tour of the UK. The team are called the All Blacks by the British press. **1906** South Africa tour the UK. **1908** Australia tour and are called the "Wallabies" by the press. They also win gold in the 1908 London Olympics, beating Cornwall in the final. **1912** South Africa tour. **1924** The "Invincibles" (All Blacks) team tour, led by Cliff Porter. They win all 32 games. **1931** South Africa booed by British rugby fans at games as they favour a kicking game instead of the typically British running game. **1936** Australians arrive and have to turn back due to outbreak of Second World War. **1947** Australia tour the UK. **1951** South Africa tour and beat all four nations plus the Barbarians. **1957** Australia lose to all four nations. **1963** All Blacks lose one game on the tour – at Welsh club, Newport. **1966** Australia inflict 23-11 defeat on England: their biggest defeat in 16 years. **1969** Demonstrations about South Africa's stand on apartheid disrupt the Springboks tour of the UK. **1972** Llanelli beat the All Blacks. **1973** Argentina tour Ireland and Scotland. Japan tour and win two out of 11 games. **1974** All Blacks tour the UK. **1976** Argentina tour England and Wales. **1979** The All Blacks win 10 out of 11 games on their tour. **1984** Australian tourists become the first Australian team to win all four games against the Home Nations. **1988** The last of the "old" tours, as Australia only play the Home Nations.

LEFT: A programme for Wales' famous victory over the All Blacks in 1905.

RIGHT: The 1905 All Blacks tour ticket, which sold at auction for £1,950.

ABOVE: The Prince of Wales presents the cup to Cliff Porter, the captain of the "Invincibles". The nickname was given to the 1924/25 New Zealand touring team. The team was one of the greatest All Blacks teams to ever tour, and they had in their squad players like George Nepia, and brothers Cyril and Maurice Brownlie. Between 1924 and 1925 the team played 32 games and won all 32, scoring 838 points and only conceding 116.

RIGHT: Welsh outside-half Cliff Morgan kicks ahead in Wales' 13-8 win against New Zealand in 1953.

ABOVE: New Zealand full-back Bob Scott beating his Welsh opponent during New Zealand's defeat at the Arms Park in 1953. Scott played 17 times for the All Blacks between 1945 and 1954.

LEFT: The Romanian rugby team after arriving in the UK for their 1955 tour. The French brought Rugby Union to Romania in 1913, and it has always been a popular sport there. On the 1955 tour the tourists lost to England and Wales. They also played Bristol, Swansea, Cardiff and the Harlequins, and made many friends along the way.

More than Just Rugby – Springboks 1969 Tour

The South African rugby team arrive for their ill-fated tour of the UK in 1969.

The 1969 Springboks tour of the UK was a watershed for South African rugby. At the time the country was in a sporting wilderness; they had been suspended by the Olympic committee in 1964 and the country had become a "no-go" area for any sporting stars who wished to play there. This was due to the apartheid system that was used to segregate the population by the colour of their skin. The South Africans had toured these shores before, in 1965, and demonstrations about their regime had been widespread but these were nothing to what was witnessed in 1969. The team were captained by Dawie de Villiers, and he famously said, "Instead of proudly stepping out at Heathrow Airport in our blazers we were smuggled onto our own coach." The demonstrations were organized by a movement called "Stop the Tour", whose leader was the now-Labour MP, Peter Hain. Also organizing the Scotland demonstrations was a young student who would go on to become prime minister – Gordon Brown. The demonstrators clashed constantly with police, and at the Swansea game alone 200 demonstrators were injured and 10 policemen taken to hospital. In amongst all this the Springboks lost to England and Scotland, whilst drawing with Wales and Ireland. The publicity surrounding the demonstrations seemed to be taken note of back in South Africa, and although things took time the apartheid laws were repealed in the 1980s, bringing South Africa out of their sporting wilderness. Their final acceptance was the triumph of the 1995 World Cup, which was held in their country, and which they went on to win.

ABOVE: Before the South Africans' match with Swansea, where 200 demonstrators and 10 police were taken to hospital.

LEFT: Police break up demonstrations before the Swansea game by people protesting against the South African tourists and their country's apartheid system.

RIGHT: Police restrain demonstrators before the East Midlands game.

BELOW: A demonstrator is led away by police during the South Africans' game against the East Midlands.

Anti-apartheid demonstrators at Twickenham before the game against England.

ABOVE: South African winger Ronnie Grobler powers through the tackle as South Africa defeat Irish side Munster in 1970.

LEFT: Cardiff v South Africa. Smoke rises from hay, which has been burned on the terraces by protesters at Cardiff Arms Park, in protest of the South African tour.

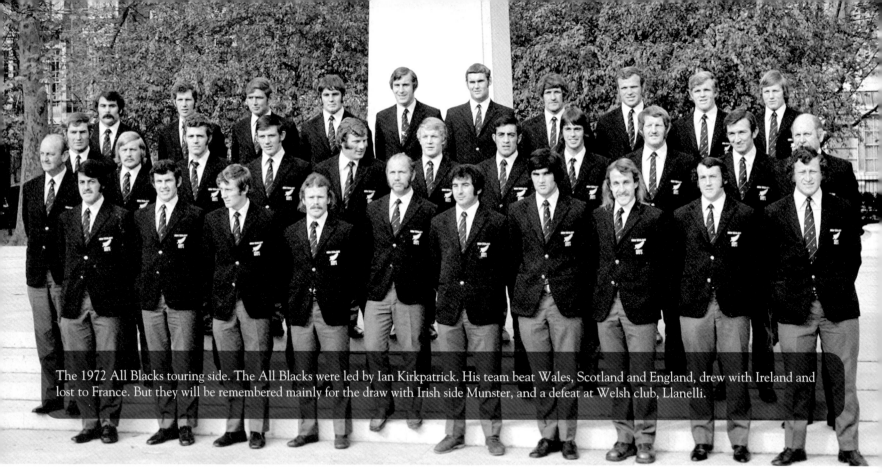

The 1972 All Blacks touring side. The All Blacks were led by Ian Kirkpatrick. His team beat Wales, Scotland and England, drew with Ireland and lost to France. But they will be remembered mainly for the draw with Irish side Munster, and a defeat at Welsh club, Llanelli.

Terry Cobner in action for East Wales, against the 1976 Argentinean tourists.

LEFT: The American rugby team, known as the Eagles. Seen here arriving at Heathrow for their first English tour in 1977. They lost 37-11 at Twickenham.

BELOW: Mark Shaw of New Zealand hands off Welsh opposition in the All Blacks' 23-3 victory over Wales in 1980.

ABOVE: The Australians win the line-out in their 19-13 victory over England in the 1984 international.

Fijian rugby players before their tour match with Scotland in 1989.

127

England captain Will Carling is carried off the pitch by overjoyed fans as England beat the New Zealand tourists' team at Twickenham in 1993. The picture shows what it meant to the fans to beat the mighty All Blacks.

Congratulations for Australian Ben Tune
after scoring in Australia's 37-8 win
against Scotland in 1997.

New Zealand's Zinzan Brooke breaks clear, as Ireland's Keith Wood bears down on him in the 1997 international.

ABOVE: Ireland hooker Keith Wood powers over the line, as South Africa's Johan Erasmus tries to stop him, in the 1998 game between the two countries.

LEFT: Jason Jones-Hughes breaks through the Puma defence in the 1999 Wales versus Argentina game.

ABOVE: Scotland's Alan Tait makes a break for the Australian line in Scotland's 37-8 defeat against the Wallabies at Murrayfield in 1999.

BELOW: England's Phil Vickery (left) and Austin Healey fight it out against the Australians in the 2000 test series.

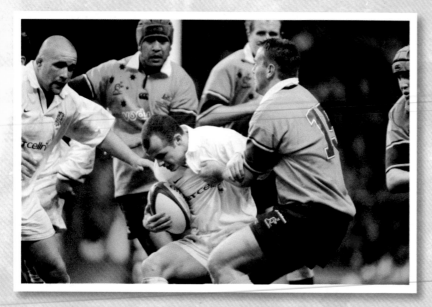

ABOVE: Welshman Jamie Roberts breaks away from the Canadian defence in Canada's touring match with Wales at the Millennium Stadium in 2008.

Best of the Bunch

There have been many great touring teams that have come to the UK. And in those sides the British rugby fan has witnessed some of the best players. Admittedly, they have been thorns in the side at times for every English, Scottish, Irish and Welsh fan. But rugby fans being the fair-minded bunch they are cannot help but celebrate some of these talents.

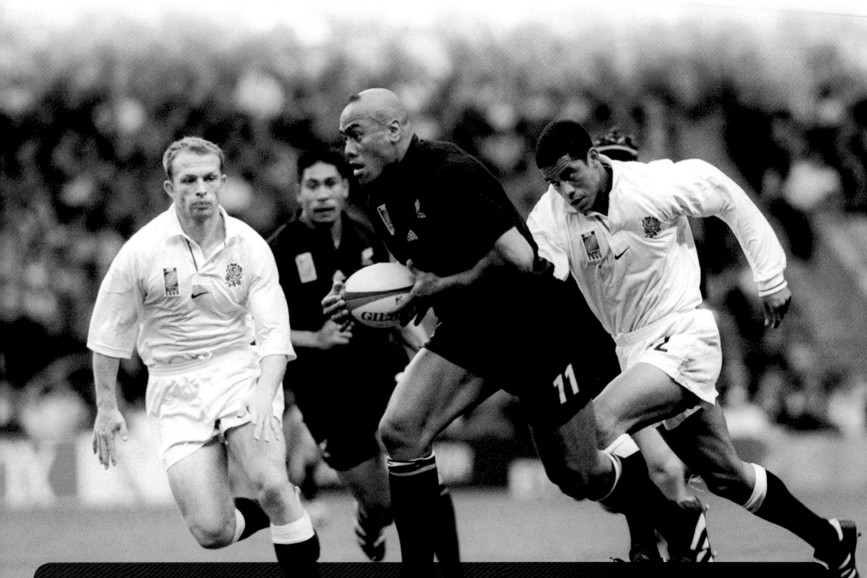

Jonah Lomu arrived on the rugby scene like a runaway freight train. The year was 1995 and he took the rugby World Cup by storm. He was powerful, strong and had the speed to go with it – which made the fact that he was 6ft 5in tall and weighed in at 19 stone ever more unbelievable. He demolished the England side as he ran-in four tries and became the first All Black since 1905 to score so many tries against England.

In 1999 Colin Meads was voted "Player of the Century" at the New Zealand Football Union dinner. It was a decision that few could argue with. This 6ft 4in New Zealand legend will always be held in great esteem by rugby fans worldwide. Legend has it that he trained for rugby by running up hills on his farm with a sheep tucked under each arm. He played 55 times for the All Blacks in numerous positions like flanker, Number 8 and lock, and his career spanned 1957 to 1971. No mean feat for an All Black.

Nick Farr-Jones lifting the World Cup in 1991.

When Nick Farr-Jones took over the captaincy of Australia the Wallabies were not at their best. Predecessor Andrew Slack was sacked after the nation's disappointing show in the 1987 World Cup. But the lawyer from Sydney certainly turned things around by winning the 1991 World Cup – putting himself right in the hearts of the Australian fans. Farr-Jones had all the attributes to be one of the game's top scrum-halves. He was strong, had a cool head and the mental toughness needed to carry a team through difficult times. He gained 63 caps for Australia and captained the side 36 times.

135

RIGHT: The legendary Serge Blanco will stay in British rugby fans' hearts forever for his graceful, powerful running skills. He excelled at everything that French rugby stood for – even if he did smoke 40 cigarettes a day. The great Gareth Edwards once said of him "Blanco is so gifted all he needs is the number 15 shirts and to be allowed to roam where he likes." It was at full-back that Blanco excelled, and his record of 38 test tries in 93 games is a testimony to his great career.

BELOW: David Campese out-sprints the opposition for another try on British soil. Campese was the Australian British fans loved to hate. It's said that he could cause an argument in a phone box, and that may be true, but nothing can get in the way of what a great player he was – and he knew it. He had a blistering pace, which caused him to rack up a record 64 tries for his country in 101 appearances. He hung up his boots in 1996 after a game against Italy. And the rugby world became a quieter place for it.

Philippe Sella (middle) was a model of consistency in France's Five Nations' exploits, with a career at international level that lasted over 13 years, taking in 111 caps. He was a complete athlete, with the ability to slice through defences due to his extraordinary turn of pace. In the 1984 Five Nations he recorded tries against all four Home Nations, becoming only the second Frenchman to attain that feat. In 1995 he joined Saracens and won the Tetley Bitter Cup final. It was the last silverware this great Frenchman won.

Who will ever forget the iconic picture of South African captain Francois Pienaar receiving the 1995 World Cup from fellow South African Nelson Mandela, after the Springboks' victory over New Zealand at Ellis Park? It was truly the pinnacle of this great South African's career. Pienaar symbolized the acceptance of this nation in the sports world, after years of being out in the cold due to apartheid. The flanker played 29 times for his country, but that moment in a South African shirt will live with fans forever.

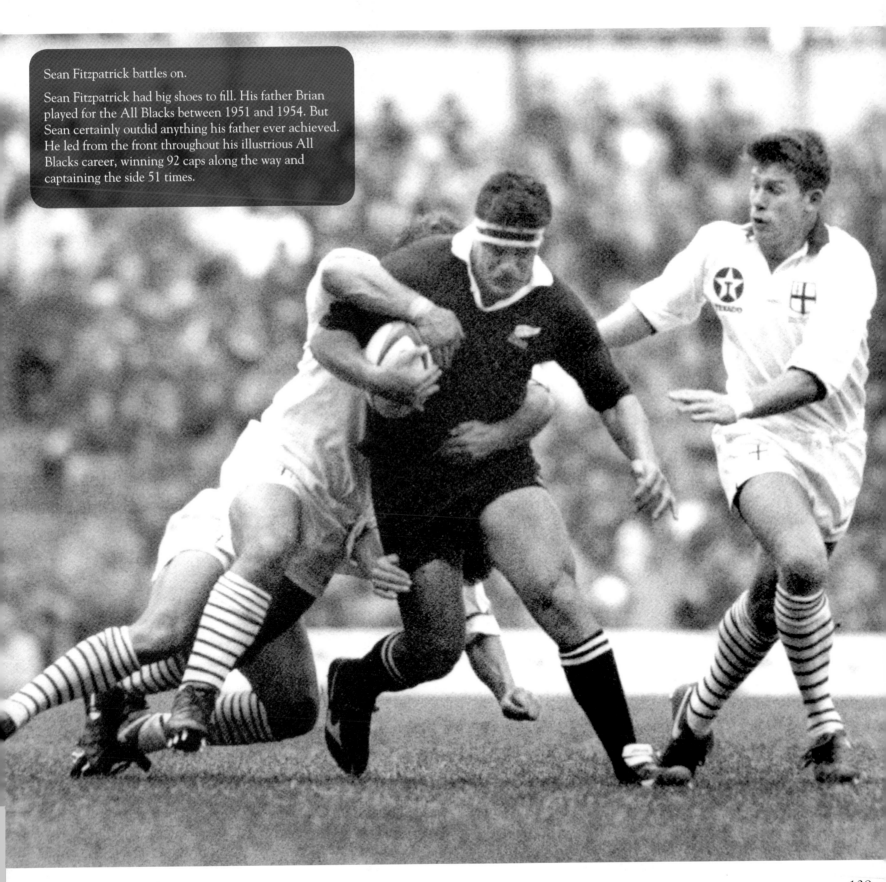

Sean Fitzpatrick battles on.

Sean Fitzpatrick had big shoes to fill. His father Brian played for the All Blacks between 1951 and 1954. But Sean certainly outdid anything his father ever achieved. He led from the front throughout his illustrious All Blacks career, winning 92 caps along the way and captaining the side 51 times.

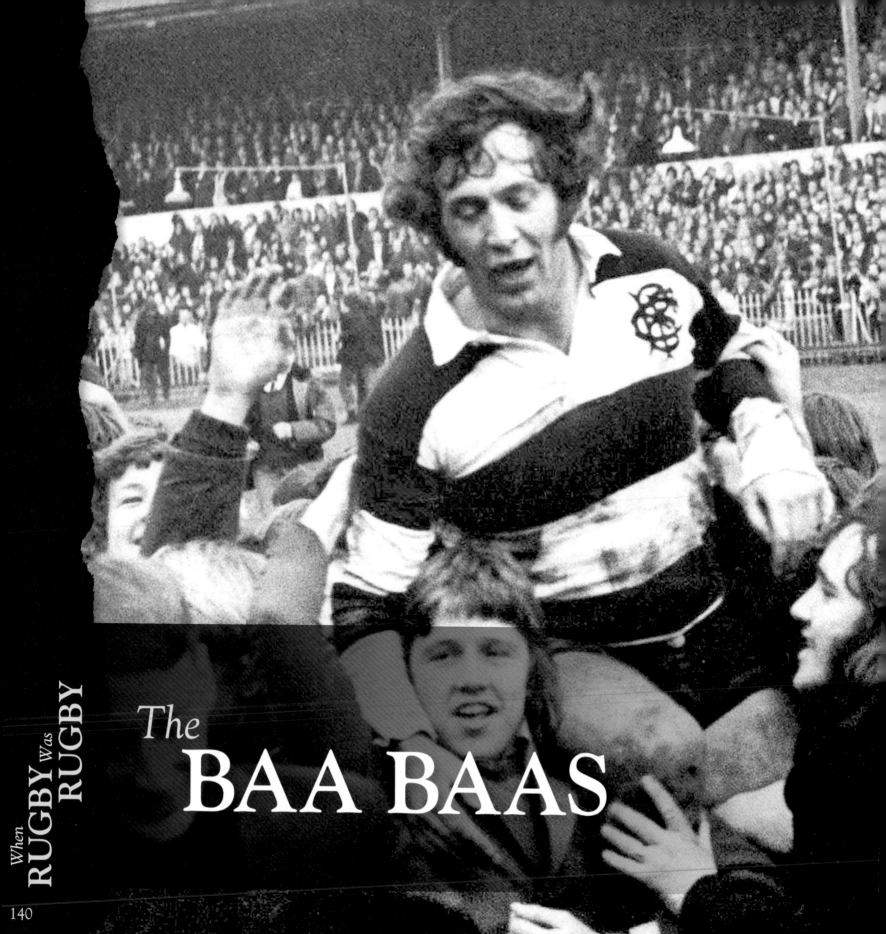

The
BAA BAAS

The Barbarians were conceived in 1890 at an oyster bar in Bradford, England. They were the brainchild of W P Carpmael, who was a Cambridge and Blackheath rugby forward. Carpmael was touring Yorkshire and the Midlands with a scratch team of rugby players. They had so much fun they decided to form a club. Their ethos for the club was that rugby should be an attacking game and the Barbarians, as the new team would be called, must always exhibit a style that demonstrated a commitment to hard, clean rugby.

To be asked to play for the Baa Baas is an honour for any player, as selection is based, firstly, on the player being of a high enough standard and, secondly, that he behave himself off the pitch. The Barbarians are unique as they have no ground, no home and are invited to play by different Unions throughout the world, with the hosts picking up the tab. Many of the greatest players ever to grace this game of rugby have worn the famous black-and-white hoops of one of its greatest traditions.

> "
> *Rugby football is a game for gentlemen in all classes, but for no bad sportsman in any class.*
>
> Walter Julius Carey
> (The Barbarians 1894)
> "

Barbarians captain John Dawes is carried from the pitch after the Barbarians' historic victory over the All Blacks in 1973.

1890 The Barbarians formed at an oyster bar in Bradford, England. First game, where they beat Hartlepool 9-4. **1891** Black-and-white hoops adopted as shirts. The Barbarians tour Wales. **1925** Club blazers, with two lambs on the badge, are issued to past and present players. **1936** Founder W P Carpmael dies at his home in France. **1948** Barbarians beat Australia 9-6 in Cardiff. **1952** South Africa beat the Barbarians 12-13. **1954** Defeat for the Barbarians 19-5 to New Zealand. **1955** Tony O'Reilly makes his debut against Cardiff, O'Reilly will go on to play 30 times for the Barbarians, which is a record. **1957** The team's first overseas tour of Canada. **1961** Barbarians beat South Africa 6-0. **1963** O'Reilly plays his final game for the Baa Baas. **1973** Gareth Edwards scores the "greatest try ever" playing for the Barbarians, as they beat New Zealand 23-11 in Cardiff. **1977** Barbarians lose 23-14 to the British Lions. **1984** Barbarians play Australia. **1990** Barbarians celebrate their centenary with a game against Wales. **2007** Barbarians beat current World Cup holders, South Africa, at Twickenham. **2008** Barbarians play Australia at Wembley Stadium. **2011** At a ceremony at Twickenham, W P Carpmael is inducted into Rugby's Hall of Fame.

LEFT: Action from the Barbarians game against Fiji at the County Ground, Gosforth, Newcastle in 1970.

ABOVE: Barbarian Rory Underwood in action against Australia in the 1984 game at Cardiff Arms Park. Australia won the game 37-30 and rounded off a Grand Slam of victories against the Barbarians as they had already beaten all the Home Nations on their tour.

RIGHT: The Barbarians in action, under floodlights, against Coventry in 1973.

ABOVE: The centenary of the Barbarians was celebrated in 1990 with a game against Wales in Cardiff. Here Paul Thorburn scores a try for Wales. Despite this the Barbarians won the game 24-19.

LEFT: Barbarians training session at Taffs Well Rugby Club before the Barbarians game against Wales in 2011. Cardiff Blues player Martyn Williams practises line-outs before turning out for the Baa Baas.

–LEGENDS–

Sir Tony O'Reilly

Today Sir Anthony Joseph Francis O'Reilly is the 11th richest man in the whole of Ireland. His personal fortune is said to be worth in the region of £1 billion. Due to his business skills and investments, Tony has become a major player in Irish society since his retirement from rugby in the 1970s. For all his international business dealings, however, to the Irish and Barbarian rugby fans he will always be known as just Tony – one of the greatest wings Ireland ever produced.

Born in Dublin in 1936, O'Reilly's rise to international rugby was meteoric to say the least. At 18 years of age he had only just broken into the Belvedere's first team when he was included in the Irish team to play France in the Five Nations. And, within a further six months, he was included in the Lions squad that toured South Africa. On his return he became a regular for the Irish, and also travelled to Australia and New Zealand on the 1959 Lions tour, where he recorded a record 37 tries for the Lions on two tours. He will always be remembered as one of the great Barbarians – with his flowing running and skill he was what the Baa Baas are all about. He played from 1955 until 1963, and his 30 appearances and 38 tries are still a Barbarian record today. There have been many stories about Tony O'Reilly, and I think the one that sums him up best is the tale about his business trip to London in 1970, when he received a shock call-up to the Irish team after being told that right-wing Bill Brown had injured himself in training prior to the forthcoming international against England at Twickenham. Accepting Ireland's offer, O'Reilly arrived at Twickenham in a chauffeur-driven Rolls Royce.

Today, O'Reilly has a wonder of riches – and so do all those fans who saw the great man play.

RUGBY –STATS–

Tony O'Reilly

Name: Tony O'Reilly

Born: Dublin 1936

Country: Ireland

Position: Centre, Wing

International Caps: 29

Clubs: Belvedere, Leicester, London Irish

Representative Honours: Barbarians, British Lions

–LEGENDS–

Gareth Edwards

Possibly the greatest rugby player of all time – that is Gareth Edwards. A supreme athlete with fantastic skill, the man from Wales was the complete rugby player. Born in Pontardawe in 1947, Edwards was a Welsh international at 19 and the youngest Welsh captain at 20; when you look at the players coming out of the Principality at that time, this was no mean feat. In the 10 years he graced the Welsh team Edwards set a world record for 53 consecutive caps, and orchestrated one of the greatest teams the sport of rugby has ever seen.

   In 1973 he had his best moment as a Barbarian when he scored the "greatest try of all time" in the international against the All Blacks in Cardiff. It is shown in a clip of film that has become grainy over the years, but Cliff Morgan's famous commentary and the Barbarians' fantastic handling and support running – where almost every member of the team touched the ball – has become a symbol of what the game is all about. The clip has become a time capsule of a generation of rugby. Edwards toured with the British Lions on the legendary tours of 1971 to New Zealand and 1974 to South Africa, and showed the southern hemisphere players what they already knew – that Wales had one of the greatest in their ranks. In 1975 Edwards was awarded an MBE. In 1997, he was inducted into the Rugby Hall of Fame, and, in 2001, he was given the honour of being voted "The greatest Welsh player of all time" at a dinner held by former players. Today he is still involved with his beloved rugby, by being a director of Cardiff Blues and undertaking various commentary roles in the sport. He will always be regarded as a symbol of a wonderful year in the game's history.

An overhead kick by Gareth Edwards on its way to touch, despite pressure from a New Zealand forward.

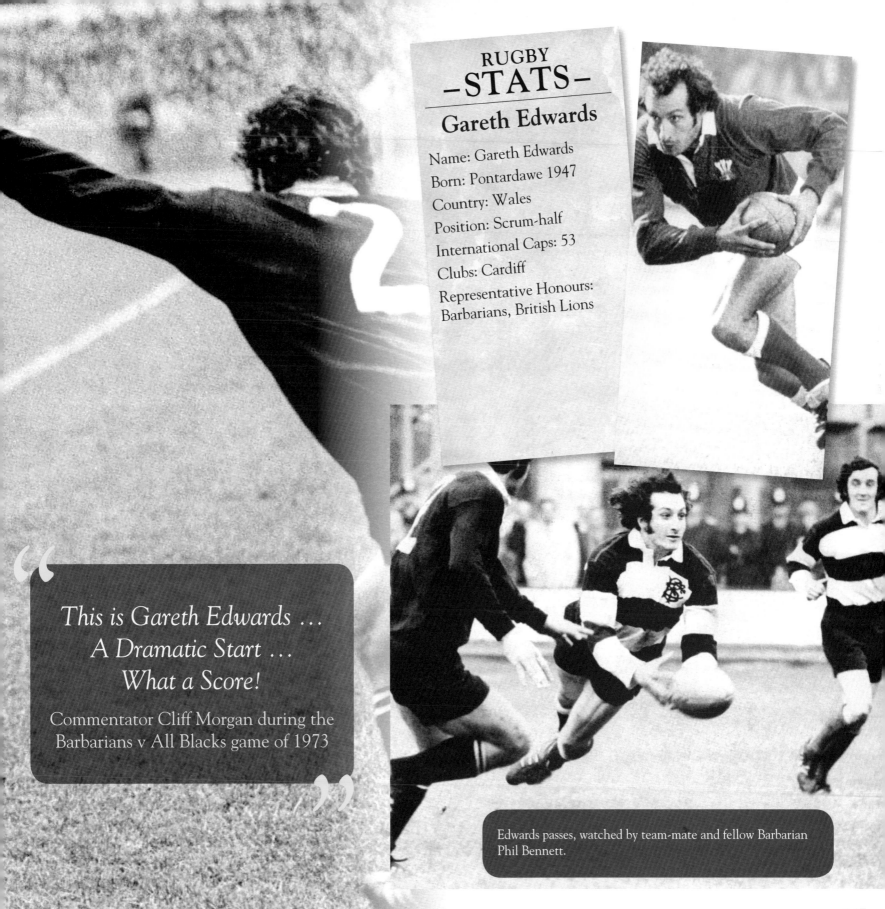

RUGBY
–STATS–

Gareth Edwards

Name: Gareth Edwards

Born: Pontardawe 1947

Country: Wales

Position: Scrum-half

International Caps: 53

Clubs: Cardiff

Representative Honours: Barbarians, British Lions

" *This is Gareth Edwards …
A Dramatic Start …
What a Score!* "

Commentator Cliff Morgan during the
Barbarians v All Blacks game of 1973

Edwards passes, watched by team-mate and fellow Barbarian
Phil Bennett.

–LEGENDS–

David Duckham

Whenever there is a debate about great players from years gone by David Duckham is seldom mentioned, probably due to the fact that Duckham was not Welsh. In fact, Duckham played 36 times for England yet only experienced victory 11 times. Loved so much by the Welsh, due to his free-flowing style, they christened the man from Coventry "Dai". Duckham was born in Coventry in 1946 and switched from centre to wing early in his career as he developed a blistering pace. He marked his England debut with a try in England's 17-15 defeat at the hands of Ireland in 1969. The tries continued for England, and so did a call-up for the 1971 British Lions tour to New Zealand. Duckham's work with J P R Williams at the back started many a try for the Lions, and he was highly regarded within the squad. After his return, he helped his club side, Coventry, to glory in the John Player Cup final in 1973 and 1974. He was then selected for the Barbarians, where he showed what he could do with an array of talent around him. His performance in the legendary All Blacks game of 1973 was an example of free-flowing skilful rugby at its best. Duckham played his last international against Scotland at Murrayfield in 1976. It ended in a loss of 22-12, which was no more than the "Honorary Welshman" was used to.

David Duckham in action for his club side, Coventry, against Bristol in the Club Championship final in 1973.

RUGBY
–STATS–

David Duckham

Name: David Duckham
Born: Coventry 1946
Country: England
Position: Centre, Wing
International Caps: 36
Clubs: Coventry
Representative Honours: Barbarians, British Lions

David Duckham (right) wrestles Australian Paddy Batch, along with England's Martin Cooper (left), in the 1976 international between England and Australia.

Fields of DREAMS

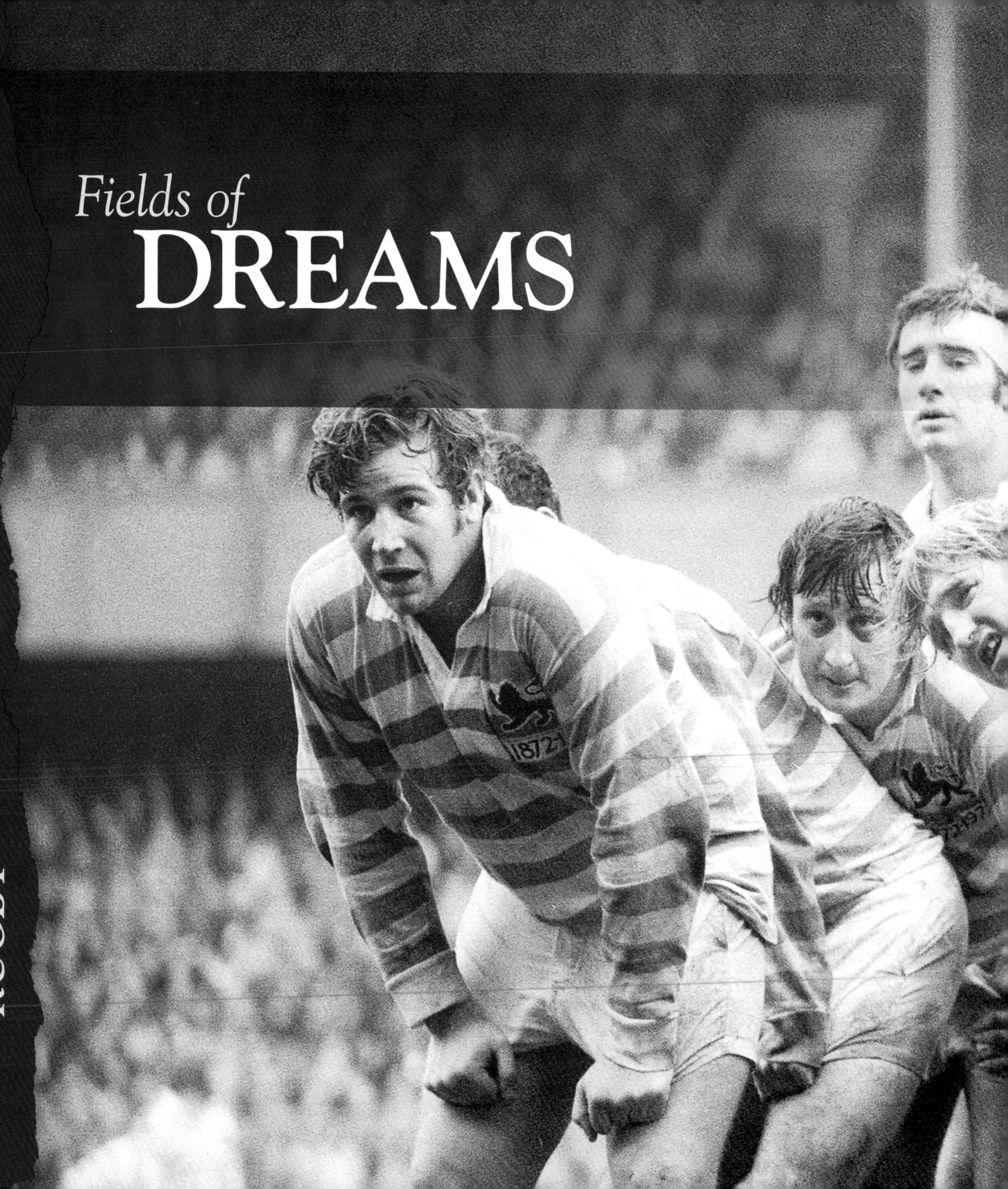

Every Home Nation has its 'Fields of Dreams'. The cauldron of noise where 50,000-plus supporters can sing their heart out in support for the 15 men lined up to represent a nation on the pitch.

Whether it's Twickenham, Millennium, Murrayfield or the Aviva Stadium, the sacred grounds have all moved in time with the game of rugby itself. These modern stadiums are now fit for a modern game, but they have lost none of the atmosphere the old grounds had before redevelopment took hold. Although, for economic reasons, each stadium holds many events such as concerts and other sports, they will always be the spiritual home of rugby for their particular nation. These grounds will, in the future, continue to provide wonderful memories for the next generation of rugby fans.

The annual varsity match between Oxford University and Cambridge University, which is always played at Twickenham on the second Tuesday in December. The fixture dates back to 1872.

Twickenham

1907 William Cail buys a market garden in Twickenham for £5,000 on behalf of the Rugby Football Union. 1908 First stands are constructed on the site. 1909 Harlequins play Richmond in the first match at the new ground. 1910 England's first game against Wales in front of 20,000 fans. 1915 During First World War the ground is used to keep sheep and cattle to help the war effort. 1921 War memorial honouring the dead is unveiled at the ground by King George V. 1927 Extension to the East Stand. 1932 The West Stand is completed. 1959 Combined team of England and Wales beat a team of Scotland and Ireland 26-17 in the centenary match at the ground. 1965 The south terrace is closed due to structural failings. 1981 The south terrace is rebuilt. 1988 Extension to the North Stand. 1995 The stadium reaches 75,000 capacity. 1999 Twickenham hosts some of the games in the Rugby World Cup held in Wales. 2000 Rugby League international between England and Australia. 2003 The Rolling Stones sell out the stadium on their world tour. 2004 New South Stand built, reaching 82,000 capacity. 2006 New seating completed for visit of the All Blacks.

RIGHT: Chauffeurs enjoy a spot of lunch in Twickenham's west car park whilst their employers watch the varsity match.

LEFT: Wales v England 1950 – and the biggest leek taken to Twickenham. It was 6ft tall and more than 18in in diameter. It went from its home in Abertillery in Wales to London via a Welsh supporters' coach.

BELOW: Cars gather in the west car park, Twickenham, before an international in 1964.

153

The Rolling Stones at Twickenham during their 2003 tour. They played two nights at Twickenham in front of a crowd of 60,000.

Murrayfield

1925 Scottish Rugby Union buy land and build stadium in the west end area of Edinburgh. First match against England. **1939** The ground is offered to the nation's war effort and used by the Army. **1944** Rugby returns to the stadium. **1975** A crowd of 104,000 – a record at the time – see Scotland play Wales. **1994** A £50-million renovation of the ground announced, including, for the first time, floodlights. **1995** NFL team the Scottish Claymores use the ground for American football. **1999** The Rolling Stones play the stadium on their "Bridges to Babylon" tour. **2000** The Rugby League Challenge Cup final held. **2004** Edinburgh football team Hearts use the ground for their European matches. **2005** Stadium hosts a Live 8 concert to help world poverty. **2007** Rugby World Cup matches played at the stadium. **2009** Rock band Oasis play sell-out gig at the ground. **2011** Rock star Jon Bon Jovi plays gig at Murrayfield as part of his world tour.

LEFT: A flooded Murrayfield in 2000. A groundsman surveys the waterlogged pitch.

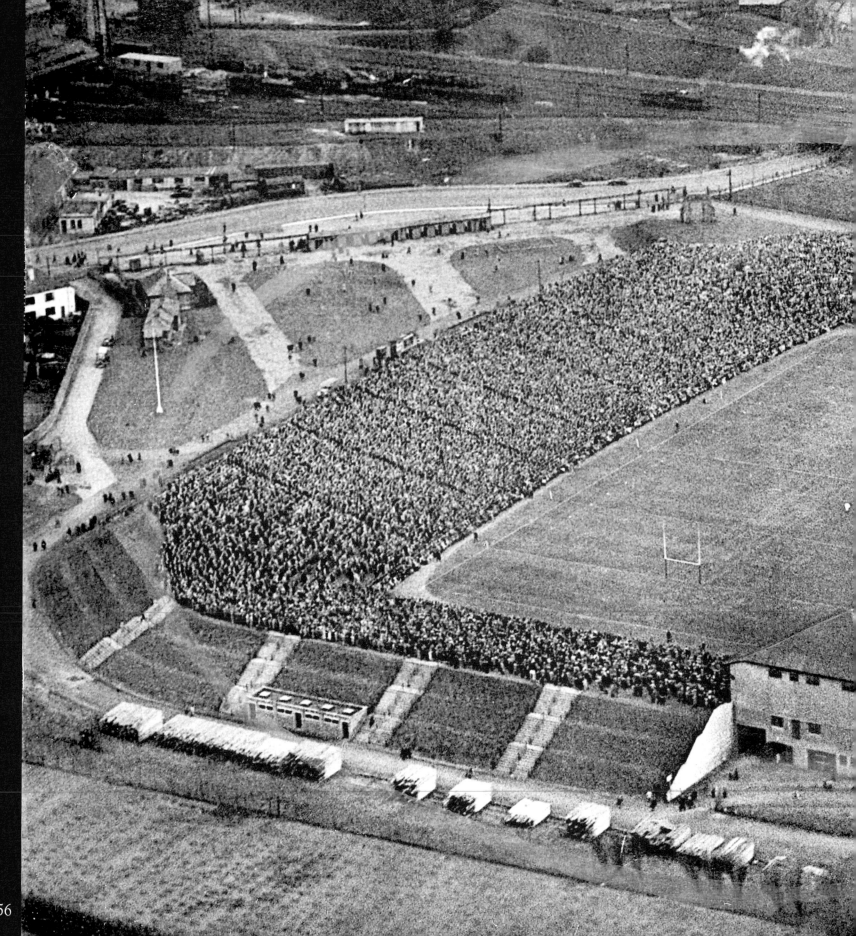

ABOVE: Murrayfield stadium during the Scotland v Rest of the World trial game in 1968.

LEFT: An aerial view of Murrayfield, from 1950.

Lansdowne Road/The Aviva Stadium

1869 Athlete Henry Wallace Doveton Dunlop has an idea to erect a purpose-built stadium for sport in Dublin. **1871** Lansdowne Road is born. **1876** First rugby match, Leinster v Ulster. **1878** First rugby international – Ireland play England. **1900** First Association Football game held at the ground: Ireland v England. **1914** 350 Rugby Union players gather on the pitch and enlist for the First World War. **1927** East Stand is built. **1930** Henry Wallace Doveton Dunlop dies. **1954** Upper Stand built, creating an extra 8,000 seats. **1971** First Association Football game played at the ground, as Northern Ireland hosts Italy. **1972** Due to the Troubles in the province, the Four Nations is cancelled. **1977** The old lower West Stand is demolished. **1978** New lower West Stand constructed. **1983** East Stand built. **1989** Frank Sinatra plays Lansdowne Road with Sammy Davis Jr and Liza Minnelli as part of a world tour. **2005** Fire in the north terrace, causing serious damage. **2006** The terrace reopens to fans. The last international played at the ground, as Ireland beat Pacific Islanders 61-17. **2007** The demolition of the ground. **2008** Rugby internationals held at Croke Park. **2009** Sponsorship deal with insurance company Aviva to name the new ground the Aviva Stadium. **2010** The 50,000 capacity Aviva Stadium opens. **2011** The UEFA Europa League final between Portugal's Porto and Braga is played on the ground.

RIGHT: The legendary Frank Sinatra, with Liza Minnelli and Sammy Davis Jr, appearing at Lansdowne Road in 1989 as part of his "Ultimate Event Tour".

RIGHT: Ronald Hakin of Ireland wins a line-out against England in the 1977 Lansdowne Road game. England won the game 4-0.

BELOW: Ireland's Tony Cascarino celebrates his goal for the Republic against England in the 1-1 European Championship qualifier at Lansdowne Road in 1992.

The Arms Park/The Millennium Stadium

1876 Cardiff Rugby Club formed, and given land by the Marquess of Bute's family for ground. **1882** Wales rugby team play games at Swansea and St Helens. **1884** Wales play Ireland at Cardiff's new ground, the Arms Park. **1905** Wales famously defeat New Zealand 3-0 at the Arms Park. Before the game the New Zealanders performed the 'haka' and the crowd responded with a chorus of 'Land of my Fathers'; it was the first time a national anthem had been sung at a game. **1933** New stand built at the Arms Park, increasing capacity to 56,000. **1954** Wales play all their fixtures now at Arms Park. **1958** Welsh Rugby Union state there is a need for a national stadium. **1964** WRU decide on the Arms Park as being their home. **1969** It is announced that a new national stadium will be built. **1970** New national stadium opens. **1977** New West Stand opens at stadium. **1988** 56,000 fans see Llanelli beat Neath 28-13 at the stadium. **1989** Wales' football team play West Germany in the first football game at the stadium. **1991** The ground holds its first evening rugby international as Wales play France at 8pm. **1993** Lennox Lewis beats Frank Bruno for the world heavyweight title at the stadium. **1997** The last international game, Wales v England, is held before the ground is demolished. **1998** Wales move their games to Wembley Stadium. **1999** The Millennium Stadium is built at a cost of £121 million. Wales beat South Africa 29-19 in the first game held in the new stadium. Wales host the Rugby World Cup. **2001** The stadium holds the FA Cup final until the new Wembley is built; Liverpool win the first final 2-1 against Arsenal. **2002** Indoor cricket match held at the stadium: Britain v Rest of the World. **2003** Rugby League Challenge Cup final held. **2007** Welshman Joe Calzaghe beats Mikkel Kessler to retain his WBO super middleweight title. Stadium hosts Rugby World Cup games. **2012** Stadium hosts football matches for the London Olympics.

ABOVE: Sheepdog trials held at the Arms Park in 1924.

BELOW: The Arms Park under water during floods in Cardiff in 1960.

ABOVE: Damage caused at the Grangetown end of the Arms Park, following a German air raid in 1941.

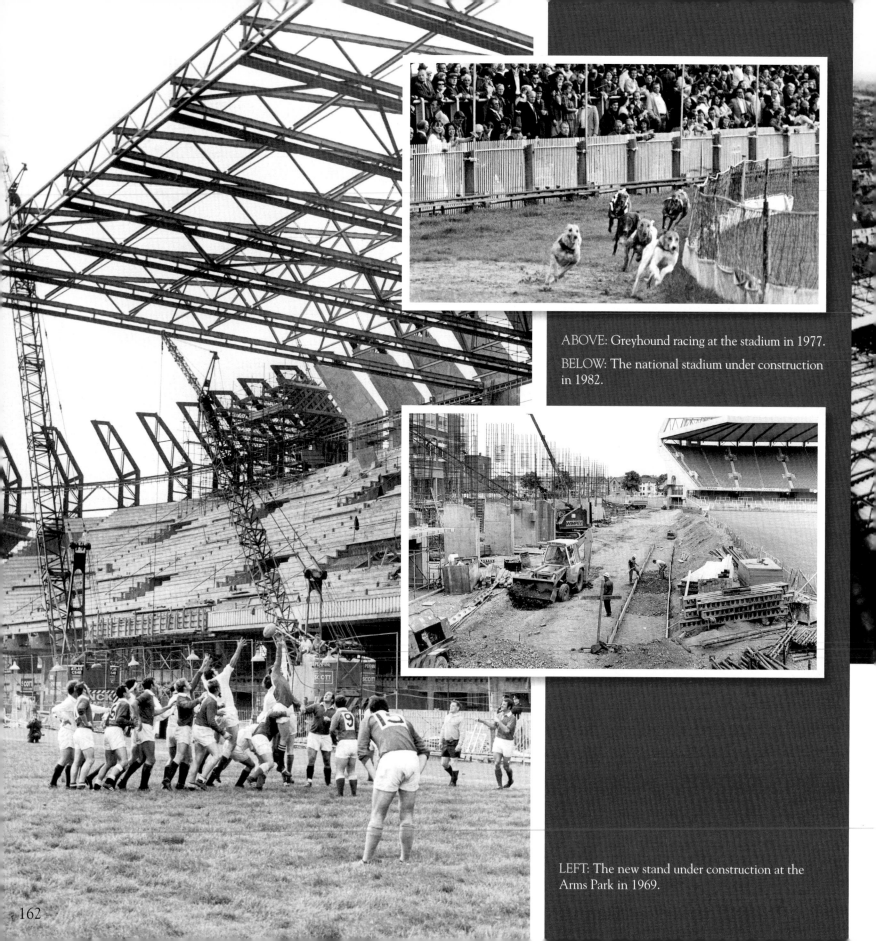

ABOVE: Greyhound racing at the stadium in 1977.

BELOW: The national stadium under construction in 1982.

LEFT: The new stand under construction at the Arms Park in 1969.

ABOVE: The Michael Jackson concert at the national stadium, Cardiff Arms Park, 1992.

LEFT: Frank Bruno and Lennox Lewis (holding the WBC Championship belt) before their fight at the national stadium. Although Lewis was born in Canada he had taken British citizenship – so the fight became the first ever world heavyweight title fight between two Britons. Lewis was the holder and he won the fight in the seventh round on a technical knockout, in front of 65,000 fans.

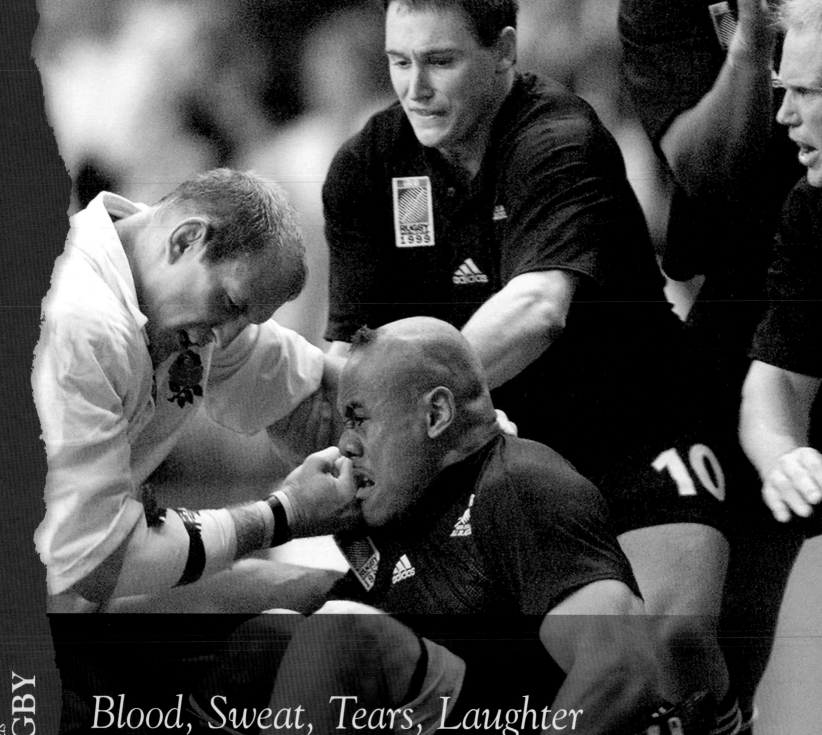

Blood, Sweat, Tears, Laughter
and ROYALS

> *Rugby is a wonderful show. Dance, opera and suddenly the blood of a killing.*
>
> Actor Richard Burton

There is an old saying that "Football is a game played by Gentlemen and watched by Hooligans and Rugby is a game played by Hooligans and watched by Gentlemen." The quote does a disservice to both games, but as far as rugby is concerned it could not be further from the truth. It has always been a sport where physical contact is a big part at any level. And injuries come and go for players. But when a rugby player stays down injured, you know it's serious. When it comes to rival supporters they can drink together and mix together without fear of trouble in the ground. On the field there is a mutual respect between players, who give their all for the cause and for team-mates. And that's a philosophy that filters down to the supporters. The game has always been "a man's" game, to coin a phrase, but, even so, hardened rugby players find it difficult to disguise the thrill of victory and the despair of failure. The game has always been a great leveller in terms of social standing. Many a public schoolboy has stood shoulder to shoulder with a lad from a council estate. The appearance of many royals at games may well have something to do with the sport's early traditions on the public school playing fields of England. But in modern times it's probably more to do with the philosophy and atmosphere, combined with the fact that rugby is a game for the people.

The rugby club atmosphere also lends itself to providing the game with many a light-hearted story – and anybody who has been on a grass-roots rugby tour will know that, "What goes on tour stays on tour." But, most of all, it's the core values of the game, which have stood since those days long ago at Rugby School, which show that blood, sweat, tears and laughs and, of course, royalty have been part of the game for years and will continue for evermore.

"Blood"

LEFT: England's Lawrence Dallaglio clashes with All Black Jonah Lomu, 1999.

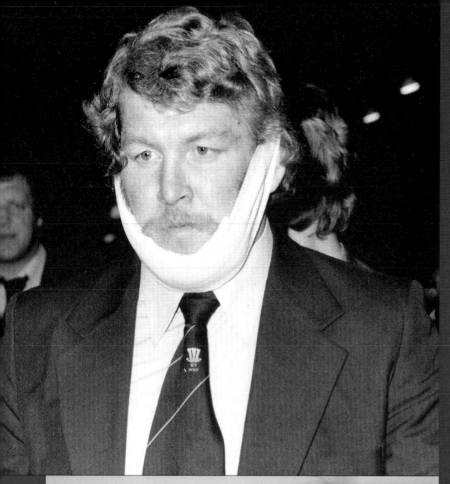

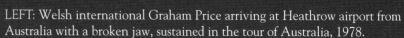
LEFT: Welsh international Graham Price arriving at Heathrow airport from Australia with a broken jaw, sustained in the tour of Australia, 1978.

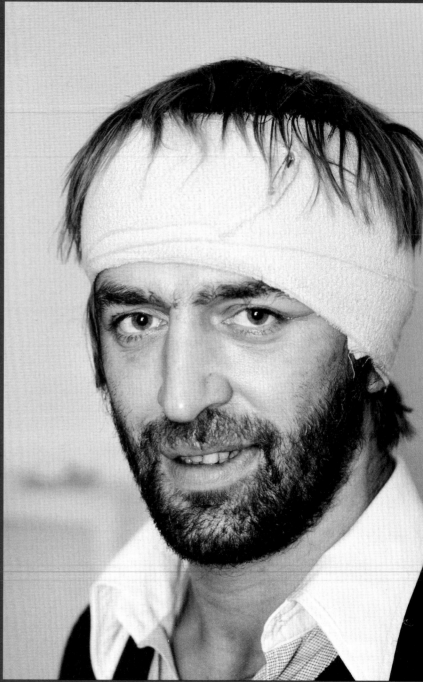

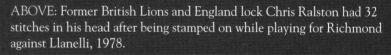
ABOVE: Former British Lions and England lock Chris Ralston had 32 stitches in his head after being stamped on while playing for Richmond against Llanelli, 1978.

LEFT: England skipper Will Carling sporting a black eye at an after-match press conference, 1996.

ABOVE: A rare photo of Gareth Edwards going toe-to-toe with Aberavon's Martin Howells during a game between Cardiff and Aberavon, 1977.

ABOVE RIGHT: Wales' Phil Bennett runs up the pitch with blood coming from his ear, 1977.

RIGHT: Welshman Mervyn Davies is carried off injured for Wales in 1972.

BELOW: England's captain Bob Hiller collapses during the Five Nations game with Wales with an injured knee. After treatment Hiller returned to the field with his leg strapped and promptly kicked a goal for England. Unfortunately it could not stop the Welsh winning 12-3, 1972.

"Sweat"

A pumped-up Brian Moore before an England international, 1991.

ABOVE: Matt Dawson (right) and Lawrence Dallaglio (left) after giving their all in a Six Nations game with France, 2000.

LEFT: An exhausted Chris Jones at the final of the Six Nations game with Wales in 2008.

LEFT: Scotland's Andy Nicholls shows the ecstasy of victory after Scotland beat England 19-13 in the 2000 Calcutta Cup.

BELOW: All's fair in love and war as a French supporter kisses a Welsh fan before the two countries' showdown in 2008.

ABOVE: The joy of victory, as Welsh captain Ryan Jones celebrates the winning of the Grand Slam in 2008.

LEFT: An exhausted Gareth Edwards, caked in mud after scoring a try for Wales against Scotland, 1968.

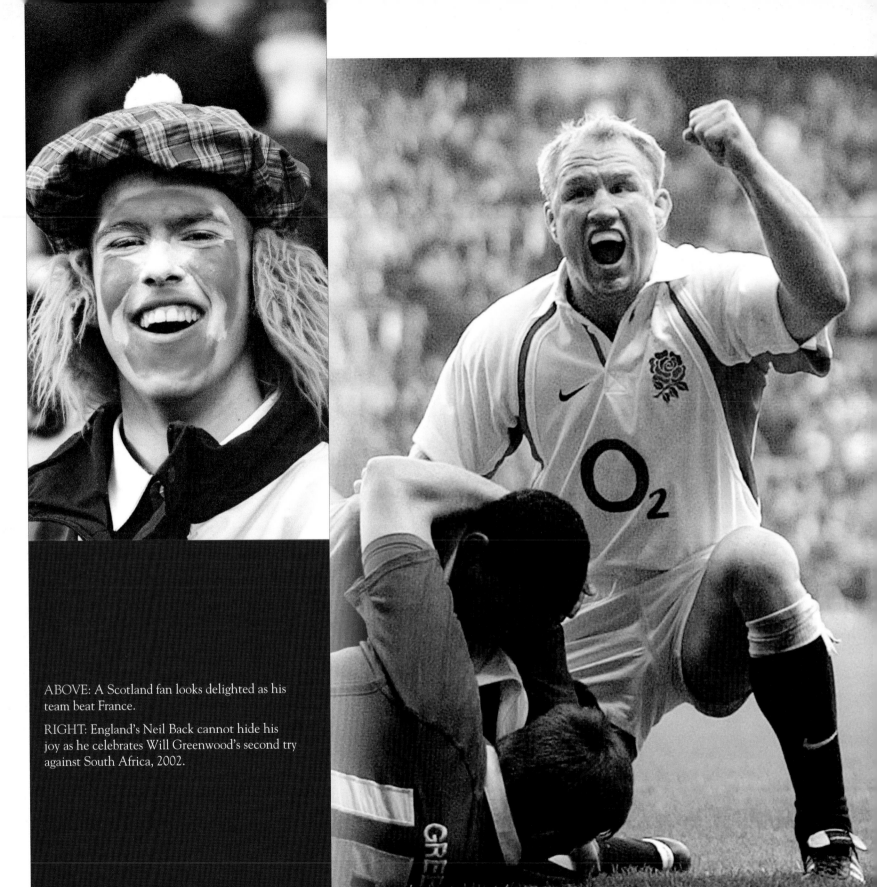

ABOVE: A Scotland fan looks delighted as his team beat France.

RIGHT: England's Neil Back cannot hide his joy as he celebrates Will Greenwood's second try against South Africa, 2002.

ABOVE: Wales' Gavin Henson celebrates at the final whistle as Wales defeat England in 2005.

LEFT: The crunch of the tackle – Wales' Stephen Jones targets Ireland's Anthony Foley minutes after kick-off in the Six Nations, 2008.

"Tears"

RIGHT: England's Jonny Wilkinson looking inconsolable after the 1999 defeat to the All Blacks.

BELOW: England coach Sir Clive Woodward after the 1999 defeat to the All Blacks.

BELOW: England players dejected after defeat at the hands of South Africa, 1999.

ABOVE: England's Lawrence Dallaglio looks a beaten man during England's 1999 All Blacks defeat. Dallaglio was a massive part of English rugby. He played 85 times for his country, as well as playing for the Lions, and was part of the England team to win the World Cup in 2003. Domestically, he won the Heineken Cup and the Championship title with his beloved Wasps.

173

Two Wales fans embrace after their team's defeat to France in the Six Nations.

ABOVE: After a defeat at the hands of England this Scottish fan can't even face leaving the stadium.

ABOVE: A young Wales fan sits alone after a Wales defeat.

"Laughter"

ABOVE: Streaker Michael O'Brien gets led off the field by police in 1974. Streaking originated in the USA and became so popular, particularly at sporting events in the early 1970s, it crossed over to Britain. American singer-songwriter Ray Stevens had a Number One hit in the British charts with a song called 'The Streak' in 1974 about the craze.

RIGHT: Erica Roe bares all for the fans at Twickenham, during the England versus Australia game in 1982.

ABOVE: A streaker is chased by a member of the Twickenham ground staff during the England and Ireland Five Nations game in 1986. You can see it's cold ... by the snow on the ground.

RIGHT: Back to the day job for Erica – working at a Peterfield bookshop. Erica will always be remembered for that "streak" at Twickenham. She later claimed she had been fuelled by alcohol and just thought "sod it". Today she lives with her husband and children in Portugal, where they produce organic potatoes on the family farm.

LEFT: England's Dean Richards (left) and Gareth Chillcott help launch the National Ballet in 2000.

BELOW: Two Welsh fans ready for the World Cup cannot hide their excitement at the Millennium in 1999.

177

LEFT: Scottish rugby fans get ready for the team's international against England at Murrayfield, 1996.

RIGHT: Pre-birthday celebrations to usher in Sean Lineen's and Gavin Hastings' 30th birthdays. (Back row) Gavin Hastings, David Sole. (Middle) David Milne, Sean Lineen. (Front) Iwan Tukalo, Scott Hastings, 1991.

"Royals"

ABOVE: Edward, Prince of Wales, (middle) and his brother, the Duke of York, (right) on their way to the Wales versus Ireland game at the Arms Park, 1924.

LEFT: Prince Harry at the England versus South Africa game, 2001.

RIGHT: Princess Anne's son Peter Phillips captaining the Scottish Schools team against France Schools. It is alleged at the toss he never said "Heads" but "Grandma".

ABOVE: The late Princess Diana joins the singing of the national anthem at Cardiff Arms Park, along with a very young Prince Harry, 1991.

ABOVE: Prince Charles with Prince Harry at the Wales versus Scotland game at Arms Park.

LEFT: Princess Anne, with daughter Zara Phillips, speaking to Scotland captain David Sole in 1991.

Prince William, with brother Harry, sings the national anthem at Twickenham, 2002.

LEFT: Prince Harry coaches rugby at Greenfield Primary School, Walsall, 2004.

RIGHT: Prince Andrew playing rugby in Canada in 1977, whilst on an exchange programme from his school, Gordonstoun. He went to Lakefield College, Ontario, for six months and joined the under-18 rugby team.

LEFT: The marriage of the Queen's granddaughter Zara Phillips to England and Gloucester player Mike Tindall, 2010. It was Scotland's first royal wedding for 20 years, and it reconfirmed the connection between royals and rugby.

BELOW: Her Majesty the Queen being introduced to a combined Wales and England team before the game against a combined Scotland and Ireland team, to mark the WRU centenary in 1980.

183

" We had salary capping. It was
called amateurism.

Peter Wheeler (Leicester, England, British Lions)

"

England's Jonny Wilkinson and Lawrence Dallaglio parade the World Cup before the Newcastle Falcons and London Wasps match.

The game of rugby has certainly had to move with the times over the years. With fans demanding modern stadiums, and TV companies splashing money around to pump into sports, rugby has had to take its place at sport's top table.

In 1987 it was announced that a World Cup competition would be set up, and this opened up the game to countries all over the world. The trophy would be called the "Webb Ellis Trophy" after William Webb Ellis of Rugby School, who is alleged to have "created" the game – typically, the Australians refer to the cup as "Bill". To date the tournament has been a fantastic event. The biggest challenge in the game came in 1995, when professionalism in the sport was introduced by rugby's governing body, a decision that went against hundreds of years of history. The change has brought about a different type of player; for example, players now are bigger, quicker and stronger without losing speed or agility. Professionalism has had its problems, particularly with rugby clubs finding it tough to meet the balance between the wages of players and income from supporters. This is a struggle that football lost many years ago; hopefully rugby will be more prudent with the influx of new money. The game at club level has expanded also, with the introduction of the Heineken Cup – a tournament for Europe's elite club sides – and the Five Nations' format has been altered to let Italy join a Six Nations competition, in a move that can only be good for the game. Rugby is certainly in a strong position to move forward towards the future.

1987 The IRB agree to hold a World Cup tournament. Trophy called the "Webb Ellis Cup". First combined tournament held in New Zealand and Australia. All Blacks win the first trophy, beating France 29-7. **1991** World Cup held in UK: England lose final 12-6 to Australia. **1995** Professionalism brought into the game. Dutch brewing giants Heineken sponsor a European trophy. English and Scottish clubs do not take part in the new tournament. French club Toulouse beat Cardiff 21-18 in the first final at the Arms Park. South Africa host the World Cup and beat New Zealand in the final. **1996** English clubs join the Heineken Cup. **1997** English club Bath beat French side Brive 19-8 in Heineken final. English clubs withdraw in row regarding how tournament is organized. **1998** Irish team Ulster beat French team Colomiers 21-6 in the Heineken final. **1999** English teams rejoin the Heineken Cup. World Cup held in Wales. Australia beat France in the World Cup final. **2000** England win new Six Nations with Italy included. **2002** France dominate the Six Nations, winning four of the next six tournaments. **2003** World Cup held in Australia. England beat Australia in the final and 75,000 fans welcome them home to London. **2007** World Cup held in France, South Africa beat England 16-6 in the final. **2008** Wales win the Grand Slam. **2009** Ireland win the Grand Slam. **2010** France win the Grand Slam. **2011** Rugby World Cup held in New Zealand, the All Blacks beat France 8-7 in the final. **2012** Wales win Six Nations.

Don't Give Up Your Day Job

With the introduction of professionalism it's interesting to see how some of rugby's top stars earned their living in the old, amateur days.

RIGHT: Martin Bayfield of England, ready to pound the beat in his Bedfordshire police uniform. Bayfield earned 32 caps for England. He made his debut for his country in 1991, and he also played for Bedford and Northampton. He retired from the game in 1996 after receiving a neck injury.

Scotland international John Jeffrey working on his farm in the Borders of Scotland. Jeffrey played for his native Scotland 40 times between 1984 and 1991. He once said of his Border farm "The only thing wrong with it is that if I go up on a mountain I can still see England."

BELOW: England's Brian Moore looking as if butter wouldn't melt in his mouth as he goes about his job as a solicitor. Moore's nickname on the pitch was "Pitbull" due to his aggressive style of play. He gained 64 caps for England and also turned out for the Harlequins and Richmond. He studied law at Nottingham University and went on to become a partner in a solicitors' firm.

BELOW RIGHT: Moore was one of the game's most passionate and aggressive players. He is seen here behind his solicitor's desk.

ABOVE: England's Fran Cotton helping team-mate Keith Fairbrother (with trolley) at Keith's fruit and veg stall in Coventry.

ABOVE LEFT: Fran Cotton carrying spuds – as opposed to rival forwards!

LEFT: Wales and Pontypool star Bobby Windsor pictured at his day job at Whitehead Iron and Steel Works in Newport. Windsor was known as "The Duke", and he formed the legendary Pontypool front row, along with Graham Price and Charlie Faulkner. He gained 28 caps for Wales and five for the British Lions, touring with them in 1974 and 1977. He was a tough player who once said, "When they outlawed punching, booting and trampling they spoilt the game."

England's Wade Dooley in his police uniform at Blackpool. Dooley won 57 caps for England and played twice for the British Lions. He was known as the "Blackpool Tower" due to his height of 6ft 8in and the fact he worked in Blackpool. When he retired from international duty in 1993, his place in the England side was taken by youngster Martin Johnson.

Six Nations

Wales celebrate the 2008 Grand Slam at the Millennium Stadium, after beating France in the last game.

ABOVE: Scotland's Thom Evans attacks, cutting through the Italian team in the Scots' 26-6 victory at Murrayfield, 2009.

LEFT: Scotland's Jason White claims a line-out in training as Scotland captain Scott Murray looks on, 2006.

ABOVE RIGHT: Wales lift the 2005 Six Nations title as captains Gareth Thomas (left) and Michael Owen (right) hold the trophy aloft at the Millennium Stadium.

RIGHT: England's Jonny Wilkinson deep in thought as England scrum down with Italy in the Six Nations, 2003.

-LEGENDS-

Jason Leonard

Jason Leonard is one of the few rugby players who transcended the professional era. Born in Barking in 1968, Leonard's success in the game reads like a Rugby Union "wish list": he has won Grand Slams in 1991, 1992, 1995 and 2003; won a British Lions test series in 1997, plus, of course, a World Cup in 2003; and played for his country a record 114 times. Despite all this he is the unsung hero of England rugby. Spotted by Saracens as a youngster, he made his England debut way back in 1990, after joining the Harlequins. The match was against Argentina in Buenos Aires. It was a baptism of fire, as the team were pelted with oranges before, after and during the game. Despite this, England ran out the eventual winners 25-12. At 21 years of age, Leonard had become the youngest prop-forward ever to play for England. Surrounded by players like Brian Moore, Wade Dooley, Mickey Skinner and Dean Richards, Leonard learnt from the best and soon became an England regular, winning back-to-back Grand Slams as well as reaching the 1991 World Cup final.

In 1993 he was selected for his first British Lions tour, in New Zealand, and in 1996 he was chosen to captain England against Argentina at Twickenham – a match in which he scored his first try for his country, and England won 20-18. The Lions called again, and Leonard was on his way to South Africa for the 1997 tour – a series they would win 2-1. Success continued with England, and, after the British Lions tour of Australia in 2001, Leonard became the first-ever front-row forward to make 100 international appearances – when he starred for England against France in the Six Nations. Later that year he would have his greatest moment in an England shirt as the World Cup was won in Australia. Leonard was awarded the OBE after the tournament, and made one more appearance for England, against Italy in the Six Nations, before announcing his retirement. His farewell game was for the Barbarians against England at Twickenham, where he ended his career with a try for the Baa Baas. In 2007 he was inducted into the Rugby Hall of Fame.

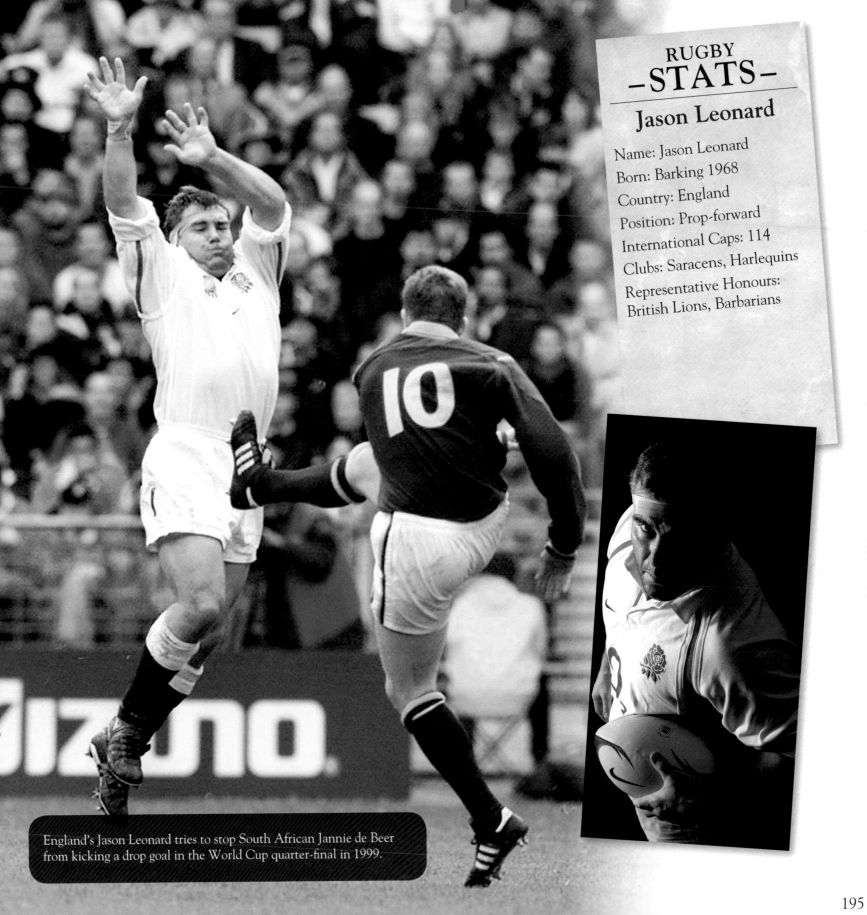

England's Jason Leonard tries to stop South African Jannie de Beer from kicking a drop goal in the World Cup quarter-final in 1999.

–LEGENDS–

Shane Williams

The very mention of Shane Williams makes you think of one word … excitement. For that is what this pocket thunderbolt from Morriston, Swansea, is all about. Born in 1977, Williams has become famous in the Welsh jersey for his sidesteps and blistering pace. It is no wonder he has been described by his peers as "One of the most exciting wingers in the world." Williams' start with the oval ball was not easy at first, as he was considered too small to play the game and instead chose football. But a desire to go in goal and handle the ball led to him arriving back in the rugby code with his junior side Amman United. He then went on to Neath, where he excelled. Williams gained his first international cap for Wales against France in 1999 – three weeks before his 23rd birthday. His first try for his country came weeks later, against Italy in the Six Nations. Part of Wales' Grand Slam victory in 2005, Williams was chosen to tour New Zealand with the British and Irish Lions later that year, setting a Lions record of five tries in a game against Manawatu.

A valued member of the Wales team, Williams won another Grand Slam in 2008, and also made his father Mark £25,000 richer after scoring his 41st try for his country against France in the Six Nations (the winnings came from a £25 bet his father had placed 10 years previously: that one day Shane would be Wales' top try scorer). In 2009 Williams was named in the British and Irish Lions tour of South Africa, and, although missing out on the first two tests, he was selected to play in the third, where he was named Man of the Match, as his two tries helped to beat the Springboks 29-9. Williams retired after the 2011 game with Australia, where he ended with a try in the closing moments of the game. Not a bad career for someone told he was too small.

"Wearing the Welsh jersey is the best feeling ever.

Shane Williams

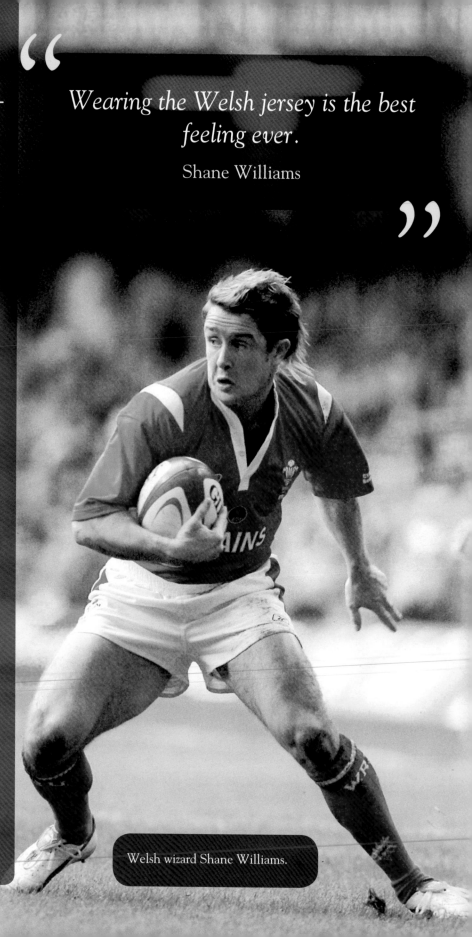

Welsh wizard Shane Williams.

Williams in action against Italy in the 2005 Six Nations Championships.

RUGBY
–STATS–

Shane Williams

Name: Shane Williams

Born: Swansea 1977

Country: Wales

Position: Wing, Scrum-half

International Caps: 87

Clubs: Neath Ospreys

Representative Honours: British and Irish Lions, Barbarians

–LEGENDS–

Martin Johnson

Things could have been so different for English rugby had it not been for a New Zealand girlfriend. Martin Osborne Johnson was born in Solihull in the West Midlands in 1970. At 19, with a love of rugby, he was spotted by New Zealand great Colin Meads and asked to try out for the King Country team in New Zealand. Johnson's trial was successful and he played two seasons for them. He was even selected for the New Zealand under-21 side that toured Australia. In 1990 Johnson returned to Britain because his New Zealand girlfriend, and later wife, Kay, wanted to travel. So Johnson joined the Leicester Tigers and a legend was born. With the Tigers, Johnson won back-to-back Heineken Cup trophies and six league titles.

He made his international debut in 1993 with a 16-15 win against France, and, later that year, was called into the British Lions squad to tour New Zealand. On his return, Johnson went on to become a massive part of England's Grand Slam side of 1995, and returned to the Lions as captain in 1997, as they toured South Africa – winning the series 2-1. Johnson became England captain in 1999, and was again asked to captain the Lions as they toured New Zealand, becoming the first man to captain them twice. With the new World Cup competition, it was always Johnson's dream to lead his country to victory – and in 2003 the dream came true as England, against all the odds, beat Australia in their backyard 20-17 – giving Johnson his finest moment. Johnson was awarded the CBE in 2004, and he retired in 2005. Inducted into the Rugby Hall of Fame in 2001, Johnson will always be remembered as one of the game's greats.

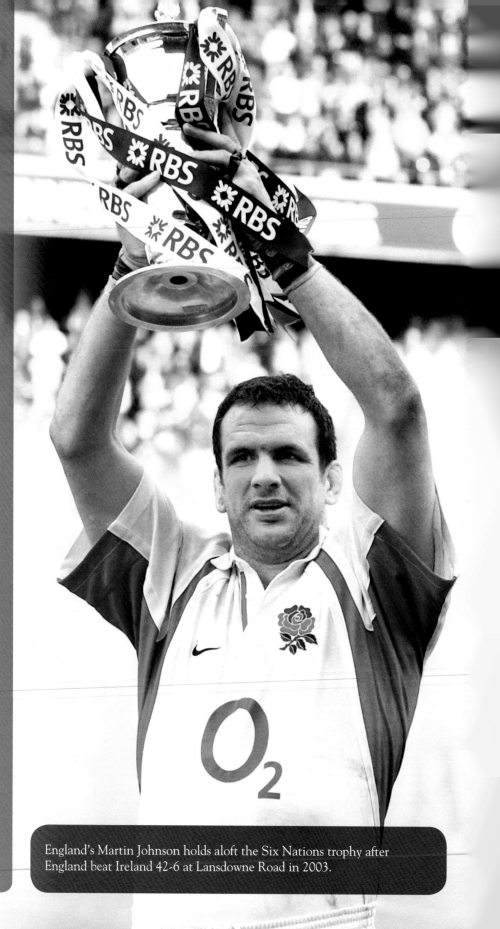

England's Martin Johnson holds aloft the Six Nations trophy after England beat Ireland 42-6 at Lansdowne Road in 2003.

RUGBY
–STATS–

Martin Johnson

Name: Martin Johnson

Born: Solihull 1970

Country: England

Position: Lock

International Caps: 84

Clubs: Leicester Tigers

Representative Honours:
British and Irish Lions

" *The best ever lock forward.*

Australian captain John Eales, 2003 "

Former rugby greats herald the new World Cup. Left to right: Ireland's Brendan Mulligan, Scotland's Gavin Hastings, England's Will Carling, Wales' Gareth Edwards, South Africa's Francois Pienaar, Wales' Ieuan Evans and Australia's Michael Lynagh.

England's Mike Tindall (left) celebrates with team-mates after England's victory against Australia in 2005.

ABOVE: England's Jeremy Guscott tries in vain to stop All Black Jonah Lomu in the 1999 World Cup group stages. New Zealand would win this contest 30-18. Lomu went on to score eight tries in the tournament, but New Zealand still lost to France in the semi-finals.

RIGHT: Scotland's Duncan Hodge holds the ball for Scotland as he is tackled by Spain's Andrei Kovalenco in the 1999 World Cup group games.

Scotland's Gordon Simpson battles through in the World Cup match against Uruguay, 1999.

England's Danny Grewcock loses the line-out to New Zealand in the 1999 World Cup group games.

Scotland's World Cup team train before the 1999 World Cup. The Scots would finish second in their group to South Africa, but eventually lose 30-18 to New Zealand in the quarter-finals.

LEFT: Wilkinson in classic pose before attempting a kick for goal for England.

BELOW: Wilkinson with the ultimate prize in rugby – the World Cup – after victory in 2003.

–LEGENDS–

Jonny Wilkinson

Jonathan Peter Wilkinson was born in Frimley, Surrey, in 1979. Even as a youngster he knew what he wanted – and that was to play for England one day. A keen sportsman, Wilkinson excelled at tennis, cricket and basketball, but it was rugby that caught his imagination. A keen student, Wilkinson took A-levels in French, biology and chemistry, and gained a place at Durham University, but he gave it up to become a professional rugby player with Newcastle Falcons in 1997. He became a permanent fixture in the Newcastle side put together by England player Rob Andrew, and, in Wilkinson's first season, the Falcons won the Premiership title.

A year later Wilkinson was picked for England – he made his debut coming off the subs bench for Mike Catt in the game against Ireland at Twickenham. He was aged 18. In 1999 Wilkinson established himself in the England set-up, and toured Australia and Canada. The 1999 season also saw his World Cup debut for England, as he scored 32 individual points in the 67-7 rout of Italy. In 2001 he was picked to tour Australia as part of the British and Irish Lions squad, and he excelled in the first test, scoring nine of the Lions' points as they beat Australia 29-13. Wilkinson did not have the best of second tests, however, as a mistake by him allowed Australian Joe Roff to score and turn the match. He was also injured, and had to be stretchered off the field as the Lions went down 35-14. Wilkinson did recover, however, and scored a try in the third test as the Lions won the series 2-1. Although dogged by injury, Wilkinson became a massive part of the England World Cup squad of 2003 and, in true "Boy's Own" style – with England level with Australia 17-17 in the final – the ball was passed out to him in the last minutes and, as the nation held its breath, he kicked a drop goal to win the World Cup. The victory broke the southern hemisphere's dominance of the trophy and made Wilkinson a national treasure. He had also become the tournament's leading points scorer, with 113 points. The team came back to England as heroes, and Wilkinson was voted BBC Sports Personality of the Year as well as IRB Player of the Year. And, to cap it all, he was the youngest ever rugby player to receive the OBE from the Queen. The following season Wilkinson was dogged by injuries, although British and Irish Lions coach Clive Woodward showed faith in him by taking him on the 2005 Lions tour to New Zealand. The tour was a disappointment for the man from Frimley as he picked up another injury. He continued to work on his game and fitness, and in 2007 he played a massive part in England's defence of the World Cup, although they were eventually defeated by South Africa in Paris. In 2009 Wilkinson moved to French club Toulon, where he is still a major player. He announced his retirement from international rugby in 2011. Jonny Wilkinson said, at the age of 12, that he was going to play for England – that's the sort of determination he showed throughout his career and that's what made him one of the modern greats of the game.

ACKNOWLEDGEMENTS

I would like to thank Richard Havers for giving me the chance to write the book and VG for recommending me. Also Kevin Gardner, Rebecca Ellis and Elizabeth Stone for all their hard work on the project.

Thanks must also go to the *Daily Mirror* for allowing me access to their wonderful archive, Haynes Publishing for making the book happen, and David Scripps and particularly John Mead, who worked tirelessly on getting the material I needed.

I would also like to thank my wife Sally, children Sophie and Jack, and all my family and friends for showing an interest in the book and giving me support. Finally, I must thank Mike Burton. Mike was a double villain to me, not only for his no-nonsense approach while playing for England against my home country of Wales but for his dogged displays for Gloucester against my team Bristol. On meeting him for the book I found him to be a fantastic character, who was generous with his time and helped me immensely with his remarkable recollections of the game. I can think of nobody more fitting than Mike to be part of *When Rugby Was Rugby*.

Neil Palmer